FULL 19 GALLO

THE
TROPICAL
FRESHWATER
AQUARIUM

THE TROPICAL FRESHWATER AQUARIUM

John A. Dawes

HAMLYN

Acknowledgements

Photographs

David Allison: pages 8 bottom right, 10, 11 bottom, 51 top left, 52 top and bottom, 53 left and bottom, 81 top, 91 centre, 93 centre, 113 top and bottom, 134 bottom; **Heather Angel:** pages 115 bottom, 123 bottom, 131 bottom; *Aquarian* **magazine:** pages 9, 93 top; **Dennis Barrett:** pages 48 top and bottom, 74, 77 top, 129 bottom, 131 top; **Wilf Blundell:** pages 81 bottom, 83 bottom, 94; **Allan Brown:** pages 12 top, 121 top, 123 top and centre, 127 top, 141 top and centre; **Bruce Coleman/Jane Burton:** pages 41, 51 top right, bottom left and bottom right, 79 bottom, 91 bottom, 103, 105 centre, 113 centre, 125 bottom, 137 centre and bottom, 141 bottom, 145 bottom; **Bruce Coleman/Hans Reinhard:** 75 bottom, 87 left and right, 91 top, 93 bottom, 133 bottom; **John Dawes:** pages 13 centre, 15, 79 centre, 85 bottom, 125 centre; **Jack English:** page 95; **Gary Harris:** page 13 bottom; **Arend van den Nieuwenhuizen:** pages 13 top, 77 top, 79 top, 88 bottom, 102, 107 top, 134 top, 143 top and centre, 147 bottom; **Anne Powell:** pages 29 left, 34, 36 left and right; **Mike Sandford:** pages 23 bottom left, 83 top and centre, 97 top and bottom, 117 bottom, 121 centre, 192 top, 137 top, 143 bottom; **Ian Sellick:** pages 11 top, 16 top, 23 top left, 29 right, 53 top, centre and lower centre, 85 top, 99 top and bottom, 101 bottom, 105 bottom, 107 centre, 109 top, centre and bottom, 115 top and centre, 119 bottom, 125 top, 127 bottom, 129 centre, 133 top and centre, 145 centre, 147 centre; **Bill Tomey:** frontispiece, pages 8 top and bottom left, 12 bottom, 14 top and bottom, 16 bottom, 23 top right and bottom right, 39, 48 centre, 75 top, 77 centre, 85 centre, 88 top and centre, 97 centre, 99 centre, 101 top and centre, 105 top, 107 bottom, 111 top, centre and bottom, 117 top and centre, 119 top, 121 bottom, 138, 145 top, 147 top.

Artwork

Linden Artists and Sue Fairhurst.

Published 1986 by
Hamlyn Publishing,
a division of The Hamlyn Publishing Group Ltd,
Bridge House, London Road,
Twickenham, Middlesex, England

Copyright © text John Dawes 1986

Copyright © artwork Hamlyn Publishing 1986

ISBN 0 600 30649 6

Printed in Italy

Contents

Introduction

Millions of people around the world keep aquaria, their level of involvement ranging from a single, solitary Goldfish in a traditional bowl to sophisticated fish-houses containing hundreds of aquaria and thousands of fish and plants.

Within the aquarium, the fascination also extends to various aspects of the hobby; for instance one person might be interested in keeping a specific species of fish, while for others the plants are the most important part of the aquarium. In between these two viewpoints lie many others, such as the 'environmental' approach in which the aquarium is considered as a complete underwater habitat where a finely balanced, interrelating community is the goal to aim for.

Whatever one's preferences may be, genuine success can only be achieved through understanding. It is, of course, quite possible (and desirable) to provide step-by-step guidelines designed to prevent major disasters. In fact, this is essential during the early days of aquarium keeping when fish, plants and aquarists are at their most critical stage. However, bare instructions will only take the aquarist so far and no further. Without some of the background information, explanations and principles, a set of rules will provide little more than temporary success and enjoyment.

In this book I have, therefore, attempted to combine a step-by-step approach with a 'principles-based' one in the hope that this will help to explain the logic behind the instructions presented. I have done so in the belief that development as an aquarist cannot occur without an appreciation of the issues that lie behind the establishment and maintenance of stable aquatic environments. I have also endeavoured to emphasise that the well-being of the fish and plants in our care must be uppermost in our list of priorities and must form the basis for all our decisions. After all, it is we who decide what conditions are going to be like in our aquaria. We, therefore, owe it to our fish and plants to pay close attention to their needs and do our utmost to gain as full an understanding of these requirements as possible. I sincerely hope that this book goes some way in fulfilling these aims.

I would like to extend my thanks to the following for the valuable discussions we have had and for their generous assistance on specialist areas covered in this book: Tom Scates and Rod Roberts of the British Killifish Association; Ian Sellick of the British Cichlid Association; Gordon Howes and Dr Keith Banister of the Fish Section of the British Museum (Natural History).

John A. Dawes

Basic Requirements of the Home Aquarium

An aquarium can mean different things to different people. For example, it can be a single container constructed predominantly of glass in which aquatic organisms can be housed. An aquarium can also be a building in which individual tanks of aquatic organisms are displayed. In between these two extremes there are, of course, numerous other possibilities. In this book, the term 'aquarium' is used in the 'single-container' sense.

POTENTIAL OF THE HOME AQUARIUM Aquaria vary enormously in shape, size, sophistication and price. However, they all share certain common qualities. Prominent among these is that, no matter how large an aquarium may be, the amount of water it can hold is a mere drop (if that) when compared to the volume of water that can be carried even by the smallest of streams. Yet, despite this drawback, the potential of the home aquarium as a source of enjoyment, knowledge and satisfaction is virtually boundless. Every aquarist will vouch for this. What other hobby can bring fishes from exotic, tropical countries right into the living room of every home, irrespective of geographic location or climate? What other hobby can provide an ever-changing living picture that never repeats itself? As a friend of mine so aptly puts it, 'There is always action – never an action replay'. And, what other hobby can provide every follower with the opportunity of making new discoveries or helping to conserve endangered species in as little as two cubic feet of water?

Keeping a tropical aquarium does all this and, as if to prove it, new clubs and societies are regularly being formed to cater for the ever-expanding needs and interests of aquarists. These range from small, local groups of enthusiasts who get together on a regular basis to exchange fish, news and views, to large national and international organisations concerned with single species or types of fish, such as Discus, Livebearers, Killifish, Cichlids, Anabantoids (Gouramis, Fighters and their relatives) and others. Many of these specialist societies also strive to maintain viable captive-bred stocks of species which are known to be under threat in the wild. In a few cases (*Skiffia francesae*, a Goodeid from Mexico, is a good example), species which have become extinct in their native waters still survive in aquaria thanks to the efforts of dedicated hobbyists. The home aquarium, therefore, when properly managed, can be many things at one and the same time. No aquarium may be able to claim equality of status with most bodies of naturally existing water, but many can lay claim to coming quite close, despite the inherent, unavoidable limitations they possess.

LIMITATIONS OF AQUARIA The fact that an aquarium is a container means that every time we set one up, we are, in a sense, encapsulating a little bit of nature and preventing it from interacting with the surrounding environment. In many cases, these little bits of nature can be extremely unnatural in that they can consist of collections of plants and animals which are never found together in the wild.

For example, a typical community tank is likely to include Mollies from Mexico, Dwarf Gouramis from India, Neons from the Amazon and a Fighting Fish from Thailand! In addition, it may contain certain types of fish that do not exist in the natural state, e.g. Lyretail Swordtails, Fancy Guppies, Golden Barbs and others. The situation as far as plants are concerned is no different, with *Cryptocoryne* species from Sri Lanka often rubbing shoulders with Water Wisteria from Malaya, India, Burma and Thailand or *Ludwigia* from the southern United States and Central America.

Even when plants and fish are carefully chosen to represent genuine geographical assemblages, the simple fact that they are brought into contact with each other in numbers that do not reflect the real situation in the wild, places them in a somewhat unnatural setting.

A further consequence of enclosing a body of water is that, no matter how large the

This magnificent aquarium has been designed to show Discus at their best. Note the separate isolated breeding tank on the far right

Luxuriant vegetation such as this can be maintained in a tank designed for small, colourful shoaling species of fish

An aquarium for Rift Lake Cichlids, such as *Melanochromis labrosus*, should have rock shelters and no vegetation

Skiffia francesae is extinct in the wild but still lives on in aquaria

aquarium may be, it cannot be expected to react to external and internal influences as a stream, river, pond or lake can do in the wild. Running water that is in constant interaction with the elements continually replenishes its stocks of essential ingredients as these become depleted and purifies itself of waste, harmful chemicals by dilution, biological breakdown and other natural processes. This, of course, cannot occur to the same extent in aquaria. Denied access to direct, overhead sunlight means that aquaria generally have to be supplied with artificial light. Although there have been spectacular advances in lighting technology, it is fair to say that no one has yet managed to reproduce natural sunlight exactly. Indeed, it may never be possible to produce a lighting unit which can actually reproduce sunlight and, at the same time, compare favourably in price with existing units.

There are other natural parameters, including water chemistry, currents, eddies and foodstuffs which cannot always find a perfect counterpart in aquaria. Since each of these can play a central role in the life cycles of fish and plants, the absence of one or more can set limits on the success that can be achieved with some species.

One of the main targets to aim for when setting up an aquarium is, therefore, to attempt to get as close as possible to the requirements of individual species or the communities in which they are kept. If this is done, then a great deal can be achieved even in modestly sized aquaria.

BASIC REQUIREMENTS OF AQUARIA

Many species of fish are tough and resilient and can often survive in aquaria which may be inappropriately stocked and/or managed. When such instances are examined

closely, it often turns out that the aquarium concerned has been set up from the human point of view.

A more reasonable approach would be to study the needs of the fish first and then set up an aquarium accordingly. In most cases, the result can be just as pleasing to the human eye and considerably more suitable for the fish.

In the wild, fish require adequate water conditions in terms of pH (acidity/alkalinity), hardness, oxygenation, purity, light and temperature. In addition, they may need shelter in the form of vegetation, rock crevices or caves. A balanced diet consisting of certain essential food items (animal, vegetable or both) is, obviously, also necessary. Further, some species may exist in large shoals while others may lead predominantly solitary lives.

Details of the principles behind these facets of the lives of aquarium fish are given throughout the book in the hope that a fuller understanding of them may lead to a deep and lasting association with fish and their successful maintenance in aquaria.

Most of the basic needs can be adequately catered for from the extensive range of aquarium hardware, foods, remedies and stocks of fish available today. Again, details of these are included in the text. Generally speaking, increased levels of sophistication are accompanied by increased efficiency. However, a great deal can be achieved with modestly priced equipment, particularly if this is combined with a caring and commonsense approach.

Although it may not prove practicable to supply every single requirement within an aquarium, we owe it to the fish to attempt to come as close to the ideal as is reasonably possible. Such attempts will usually result in healthy fish and a happy fishkeeper.

9

The Main Characteristics of Aquarium Fish and Plants

A well-established aquarium will harbour a wide variety of living organisms. These will range from minute, microscopic bacteria and (perhaps) viruses to large, macroscopic organisms, such as snails, plants and fish.

Some of these will lead predominantly independent lives, relying largely on raw materials available in the surrounding environment. Most plants will fall into this category. Other tank occupants, including fish, will act as unwilling hosts to parasites and as unwitting hosts to essential, beneficial micro-organisms, such as those that live in the gut which help break down plant cells into a digestible form.

Strictly speaking, therefore, it is wrong to consider an aquarium as housing only fish and plants. These two types of organisms are, however, the most evident, and it is well worthwhile taking a look at some of their main characteristics.

MAIN CHARACTERISTICS OF FISH There are considerably more than 20,000 species of fish known to science, occupying an amazingly wide range of habitats, from the frozen waters of the Poles (where a biological 'anti-freeze' is required to keep the blood flowing) to the steaming waters of thermal pools. Yet, despite the great diversity of sizes, shapes, colours and metabolic adaptations that exists, all true fish have certain things in common. I have used the term 'true fish' because there is another group which is frequently and misleadingly included with them but which, according to some authorities, should not be regarded as fish at all. These are the Agnathans, otherwise known as the Jawless Fishes or Cyclostomes, and represented by the well-known Lampreys and the less well-known Hagfishes.

Although Agnathans look superficially like eels and possess certain fish-like characteristics, they may be distinguished from the Gnathostomes, the Jawed or True Fishes, in a number of fundamental ways. For example, in addition to lacking a jaw, Agnathans also lack a complete backbone, gill slits (they have pores), possess two (rather than three) semi-

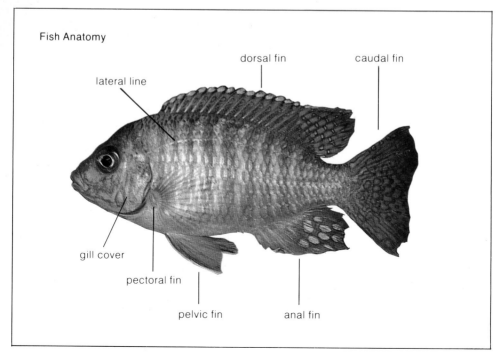

Fish Anatomy

lateral line

dorsal fin

caudal fin

gill cover

pectoral fin

pelvic fin

anal fin

circular canals in the ear, and have internally directed gill elements which are fused to the base of the braincase or neurocranium. Further, fossil evidence appears to indicate that the ancestral lines of modern-day Agnathans and Gnasthostomes separated very early in geological time, probably around 500 million years ago.

Returning to the True Fishes living today, these can be subdivided into two main categories, the Cartilaginous Fishes (Chondrichthyes) represented by Sharks, Rays and Chimaeras, and the Bony Fishes (Osteichthyes) represented by all the rest. As far as the tropical freshwater aquarium is concerned, the vast majority of species kept fall in the second group. The few Cartilaginous Fishes kept are usually Stingrays, such as *Potamotrygon laticeps* from the Amazon Basin. Needless to say, these fish are not often encountered in the hobby and are best left to the specialists. Bony Fishes can be identified by a combination of the following characteristics:

1. They possess a braincase, backbone and 'limb' skeleton consisting, at least partly, of bone.
2. They possess fins, usually containing spines, rays or a combination of both (but extreme modification may occur).
3. They breathe through gills which are externally directed and which are generally covered with gill plates (opercula) which result in an external slit-like opening in most species (eels are exceptional).
4. The body is covered with scales in most species. In some, these may be modified into hard protective plates, as in the Armoured Catfishes (families Callichthyidae and Loricariidae), including the well-known *Corydoras* and *Loricaria* species. In others, scales may be absent altogether. Catfish belonging to the family Pimelodidae are good examples.
5. They possess an air-filled sac known as the swimbladder used largely in buoyancy control. This may be highly modified or secondarily lost, as in bottom-living species like the Sucking Loach (*Gyrinocheilus aymonieri*).
6. They possess a sensory lateral line which may be single and run the whole length of the body, split into anterior and posterior portions located at different heights, or highly reduced and restricted.
7. They are poikilothermic (cold-blooded). This means that the temperature of the blood changes with and closely matches that of the surrounding water.

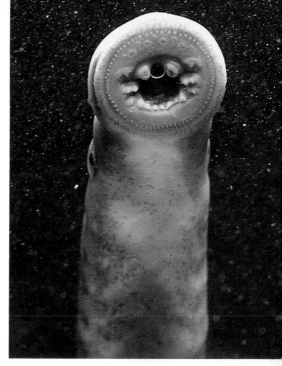

The rasping teeth of this Lamprey are clearly visible. Despite their appearance, Lampreys are not true fish

Many Catfish, such as this Panaque, have their scales developed into strong armour plating

If the list of characteristics appears to be somewhat lengthy and longwinded, it is merely a true reflection of the wide diversity of forms that exists among fishes. While this may make it difficult to define precisely what a fish actually is in simple, categorical terms, it also means that the permutations on shape, size, colour, and metabolic and behavioural adaptations are virtually endless. One just has to consider the ever-expanding catalogue of varieties that have been and are being developed from the basic, short-finned, wild form of the Guppy (*Poecilia reticulata*) to begin to get an idea of the magnitude of this diversity. It is, therefore, hardly surprising that the hobby of fish-keeping attracts countless millions of enthusiasts worldwide.

Although this book is restricted to tropical freshwater aquarium fish, the range available to the hobbyist is almost unbelievable. Taking size as the main criterion, the range extends from tiny species, such as *Heterandria formosa* (about the seventh smallest vertebrate known) to giant species like the Arapaima (*Arapaima gigas*) from the Amazon which can grow to more than 2 metres (6 ft) in length.

Colourwise, there are transparent species, such as the Indian Glassfish (*Chanda ranga*) and the Glass Catfish (*Kryptopterus bircirrhus*), on the one hand and the brilliant Killifishes, like the various *Aphyosemion* species, or the African Rift Lake Cichlids, on the other.

In terms of feeding habits, there are predatory species like Snakeheads (*Channa* and *Ophicephalus*), Tiger Fish (*Hoplias*

Aphyosemion gulare is just one of many spectacular Killifishes whose brilliant colours almost defy description

When it comes to beautiful sail-like finnage few, if any, fish can outdo *Poecilia velifera*, one of the Sailfin Mollies

Heterandria formosa, a species of Mosquito Fish, is one of the smallest vertebrates (back-boned animals) known

In stark contrast to *Heterandria formosa*, *Arapaima gigas* (from the Amazon) is the largest freshwater fish (up to 3 m)

Snakeheads, i.e. *Channa* and *Ophicephalus* species, are sleek, efficient predators, some of which grow to over 1 m

malabaricus) and Piranha (*Serrasalmus*), or herbivorous grazers like the Plecostomus (*Hypostomus* spp) and the Bristle-nosed Catfish (*Ancistrus* spp).

Turning to finnage, there are the elegant, delicate, flowing fins of Angelfish (*Pterophyllum scalare*), particularly the aquarium-bred strains, the short, sturdy fins of the Goodeids (Mexican Livebearers), the hairlike, sensory pelvic fins of some Gouramis, the sail-like dorsal fins of some of the Mollies (*Poecilia latipinna* and *P. velifera*) and every possible configuration in between.

The diversity in behaviour is equally wide, ranging from responses to members of the same species or sex (or to those of a different species or sex), to light or darkness, to differences in breeding behaviour (e.g. the production of eggs or their retention within the body cavity) and every other aspect concerning

the survival of the species. This will involve communication between individuals by any and every means available, including posture, changing coloration, sounds and, even, electricity.

Unlikely though it may seem, much of the above can be observed in home aquaria. Admittedly, special provision has to be made in the case of very large or demanding species. Indeed, in such cases, only a limited range of the overall spectrum of characteristics of these species can be fully appreciated (e.g. it is, clearly, next to impossible to provide suitable accommodation for the successful breeding of *Arapaima*).

Where easier, smaller species are concerned, the potential is considerably greater, as long as certain factors are given careful consideration. Although *every* aspect of fish biology is important, in practice, there are three main areas which, if suitably catered for, will virtually ensure that maximum enjoyment and knowledge are derived from the keeping of fish. These are: 1 Nutrition; 2 Health; and 3 Reproduction. Because of their fundamental importance, each of these topics will be dealt with at some length later on.

MAIN CHARACTERISTICS OF PLANTS
The plant kingdom is represented by countless species worldwide. Generally speaking, plant cells can be easily distinguished from animal ones in a number of ways, some of which are outlined in the accompanying table:

Plant Cells	Animal Cells
Possess rigid cell walls plus a flexible cell membrane.	Lack a cell wall but possess a flexible cell membrane.
Tend to have a prominent, central fluid-filled space (vacuole).	Often lack prominent vacuoles.
Generally lack centrioles (which play a part in animal cell division).	Usually possess two centrioles.
Late stages in cell division include the formation of a cell plate between the two new (daughter) cells.	Late stages in cell division include 'pinching' to produce the two daughter cells.
Generally non-motile (i.e. lack ability to move).	Generally motile.
Can contain chloroplasts (green, pigment-containing structures).	Nearly always lack chloroplasts.

Cabomba aquatica has delicate yellow flowers not often seen in aquarium-reared specimens

A creatively arranged aquarium provides a pleasing aquascape worthy of a privileged position in any home

As can be seen from these details, some of the characteristics appear not to be clear-cut. The reason for this is that, remarkable though it may seem, the line that separates plants from animals is extremely difficult (perhaps impossible) to draw accurately.

For example, chlorophyll is a pigment that allows green plants to synthesise food from sunlight, carbon dioxide and water in a complex series of reactions known as photosynthesis (see page 18 for further details). It would, therefore, seem logical to regard any cell which contains chlorophyll as a plant cell. However, plant cells do not swim! Or do they? There are, in fact, quite a few single-celled organisms which possess this typically animal property yet, at the same time, contain chlorophyll and are quite capable of photosynthesising. Are these organisms to be regarded as plants or animals? Clearly, this question is easy to pose but incredibly difficult to answer comprehensively. The result is that some leading authorities consider such organisms as algae (plants) while others regard them as protozoa (single-celled animals).

In this book I have chosen the former option, which gives the ability to photosynthesise greater significance than all other properties. I have, consequently, referred to those disease-causing micro-organisms which possess the photosynthetic quality as algae in the relevant paragraphs of the chapter on Fish Health. Fortunately, the majority of plants *can* be distinguished from animals quite easily.

Plants can be divided into two large groups, the Non-green Plants and the Green Plants. The Non-green Plants include fungi and moulds, the best-known types being mushrooms and toadstools, yeasts (used in fermentation) and, in the aquarium hobby, those that cause Cottonwool or Fungus disease in fish (e.g. *Saprolegnia*).

The Green Plants include algae, liverworts, mosses, ferns, conifers and flowering plants. Lichens, which are joint organisms in that they consist of an alga (usually blue-green or green) and a fungus living in a mutually beneficial relationship known as symbiosis, constitute yet another group that is difficult to classify. Mosses are represented in aquaria by a few species, e.g. Willow Moss (*Fontinalis antipyretica*) in coldwater aquaria and Java Moss (*Vesicularia dubyana*) in tropical ones. Among the liverworts, only *Riccia fluitans* is ever encountered with any regularity in tropical aquaria. The most popular ferns are *Ceratopteris* spp. (Indian Fern), *Microsorium pteropus* (Java Fern), *Salvinia* spp. and *Azolla caroliniana* (Fairy Moss – it is a fern despite its common name).

Flowering plants are, by far, the most common form of aquatic vegetation cultivated in home aquaria. Numerous species are easily available at very reasonable prices though by no means all flower with any regularity. In addition, many of those that do, have small inconspicuous blooms whose considerable fragile beauty can only really be appreciated at close quarters. Because of this, aquarium plants are generally chosen for their photosynthetic ability, the beauty of their foliage, the shelter they undoubtedly afford the fish and their buffering (cushioning against rapid change) and purifying qualities.

The ability of plants to purify is often overlooked, yet it can play a significant role, particularly in aquaria that are inadequately filtered or maintained. By absorbing certain chemicals (some of which are toxic waste products generated by the fish themselves), plants can play an important part in keeping the water in a healthy, balanced state. This undoubtedly helps in preventing potentially abrupt, harmful fluctuations in water quality.

Fish Nutrition

While it is often said, perhaps with a certain degree of justification, that some humans live to eat, the opposite is even truer of fish – they eat to live. Food is, therefore, predominantly functional in fish, even though many species or individuals demonstrate a distinct preference for one particular type of food.

In the wild, much time and energy is spent searching for food. In the aquarium, where fish are faced with artificial conditions, including food items that they never encounter in the wild, their feeding behaviour can sometimes be quite different to that encountered in nature. Even so, much can be learned about fish and their diets through patient observation.

Some fish are predominantly or exclusively herbivorous, e.g. Sucking Loaches (*Gyrinocheilus aymonieri*) or any of the Plecostomus species (*Hypostomus* spp), while others, such as most Piranhas (*Serrasalmus* spp) or the Tiger Fish (*Hoplias malabaricus*) are highly carnivorous or piscivorous (fish eaters). Some fish are even parasitic, feeding off the tissues of other fish or any terrestrial animal that happens to cross their path. Many of the Parasitic Catfishes (Family: Trichomycteridae), represented by species like the Carnero or Candiru (*Vandellia cirrhosa*), fall into this category.

In between these extremes, there exists a wide variety of feeding techniques and adaptations. Some of these are extremely specialised, like the proboscis-like, extended lower jaw of the Elephant-nosed Fish (*Gnathonemus petersi*), while others can exploit a range of food items. Gouramis, for example, will take food from the surface, middle or bottom layers of the water and will feed on live or dead plant and animal matter. Such fish are said to be omnivorous.

Anatomically, there are numerous features which give an indication of the preferred diet of a particular fish. Many of these follow the same rules that apply for land-living animals. For example, herbivorous fish have a long, convoluted gut, while carnivores/piscivores have a much shorter one. Fish which are regarded as food items by larger predators have evolved predator-avoidance features which can be anything from a highly developed shoaling instinct to camouflage or the ability to swim at a faster rate than the hunters themselves, plus every other conceivable possibility.

Eating, or the avoidance of being eaten is, quite clearly, a full-time occupation. Its importance is such that it is only temporarily relegated to second place in times of aggression or reproductive activity.

Essential Components of a Healthy Diet

Despite the diversity of strategies and adaptations found in fish, the aim of feeding remains the same in all cases: to obtain the basic nutritional requirements necessary for

Euchilichthys guentheri has the pad-like dentition typical of species whose diet consists largely of encrusting algae

The Tiger Fish, *Hoplias malabaricus*, living up to its name and formidable reputation

Gnathonemus spp. (probably *tamandua*) has a long, proboscis-like mouth well suited to searching in mud/sand for hidden food

growth and survival. Failure to do so will, obviously, result in death. These basic nutritional requirements are just as complex and varied in fish as they are in humans and fall into the same categories: proteins, fats/oils, carbohydrates, vitamins and minerals.

Proteins Proteins are large organic molecules needed by living organisms to perform a host of metabolic processes such as those involved in digestion, growth and reproduction. Although all fish need proteins, young individuals require a higher concentration than adults in their diet. All proteins are characterised by the possession of the essential element, nitrogen.

The Nitrogen Cycle Relatively few organisms can utilise, or fix, nitrogen directly from the air, but those few that can (largely, certain species of bacteria and algae) are present in astronomical numbers. Some nitrogen will, therefore, reach the aquatic environment directly, by fixation. Other supplies arrive indirectly by means of terrestrial plants and animals which may die in, or be washed into, streams, rivers, lakes or any other bodies of water. In various ways, nitrogen will get into the water. Plants take up some of this nitrogen and incorporate it into their own tissues, while many animals, including some fish, obtain their nitrogen, in turn, by eating vegetation. Other fish then feed on these herbivores (or on carnivores/piscivores which eat herbivores) and, in so doing, receive their own supply of nitrogen.

Once consumed, nitrogen is destined to be

incorporated into the consumers' own proteins. First, the nitrogen-carrying compounds are broken down by a series of enzymes (which are, themselves, proteins) into individual nitrogen-rich units called amino acids. Once this process has been completed, a different series of enzymes assembles the amino acids into new proteins, characteristic for the species in question.

One of the waste products generated by fish is ammonia. This nitrogen-containing substance is highly toxic. Clearly, any toxicity needs to be neutralised quickly in some way or other, particularly in the close confines of an aquarium. The process of neutralisation is known as nitrification. The first step involves the conversion of ammonia to somewhat less toxic nitrites by bacterial action. The best-known group of bacteria associated with this stage are those belonging to the genus *Nitrosomonas*. Bacteria of a different genus, *Nitrobacter*, carry the process a step further by converting the nitrites into relatively harmless nitrates. This last group of chemicals almost marks the completion of the cycle in that (as nitrates) nitrogen once more becomes available to plants. This, in fact, is the form in which it was originally taken in 'at the top end of the nitrogen conveyor belt'.

The final major piece in the jigsaw is provided by a range of decomposing bacteria which release nitrogen into the environment through the denitrification of dead organisms.

Fats/Oils (Lipids) Fats act as the main source of energy in fish (although carbohydrates also play a major role in this). If a fish receives a well-balanced diet in terms of fats, it can utilise a higher percentage of proteins in growth or in the building and repairing of tissues. If, on the other hand, the diet is lacking in fats and carbohydrates, some proteins will be used as alternative energy sources. In addition to their role as an energy source, fats also form essential components of cell membranes and, therefore, play a part in creating new tissues.

From the dietary point of view, fish flesh is relatively rich in fats, while plant tissues contain considerably less. Not surprisingly, therefore, carnivorous/piscivorous species of fish exhibit faster growth rates than omnivores or herbivores.

Fats also perform an important role in that they can be stored and utilised during periods of food scarcity. If, however, too much fat is present in a fish's diet, it will deposit some of the excess, mainly in the liver and around the kidneys and heart. This will then adversely

Pike, Carp, living plants, decaying vegetation and bacteria are just some of the vital components of the Nitrogen Cycle

$$CO_2 \quad + \quad H_2O \quad \xrightarrow[\text{Light (Energy)}]{\text{Chlorophyll}} \quad CH_2O \quad + \quad O_2$$

(Carbon dioxide)   (Water)   (Carbohydrate)   (Oxygen)

$$CH_2O \quad + \quad O_2 \quad \xrightarrow{\text{Respiration}} \quad CO_2 \quad + \quad H_2O \quad + \quad \text{Energy}$$

(Carbohydrate)   (Oxygen)   (Carbon dioxide)   (Water)

affect the health of the fish and can lead to serious disorders or, in extreme cases, death. At the other end of the scale, lack of essential fat-derived food components (fatty acids) have been linked with diseases such as Fin Rot.

Some fish incorporate a relatively large amount of fat or oil in their eggs. This is usually associated with species which produce floating eggs. Gouramis, like the Dwarf (*Colisa lalia*) and Pearl (*Trichogaster leeri*), fall into this category. Small droplets of lipid can often be seen floating on the water surface as the eggs of these species begin to hatch. The rest is retained within the yolk sacs of the hatchlings which, consequently, float upside-down until this energy store is used up.

Carbohydrates Carbohydrates are organic molecules of variable size, characterised by the possession of carbon (C), hydrogen (H) and oxygen (O). The primary role of this group of substances is to act as 'fuel' which, when oxidised during respiration, releases the energy required for metabolic processes to take place, such as the building up of proteins from amino acids (see diagram on page 17).

The Carbon Cycle Carbon dioxide is a highly soluble gas. Therefore, given a situation in which the concentration of carbon dioxide in solution is less than that in the air, some molecules of the gas will pass into solution. If, however, the carbon dioxide content of the water is higher than that of the surrounding air, the movement of molecules will be in the opposite direction. Both types of transfer are enhanced by agitation of the water surface, as occurs in flowing water-courses, standing bodies of water during windy conditions or, in the case of aquaria, when airstones, under-gravel filters or spray-bar power filter attachments are used.

Although carbohydrates are such vital compounds, animals cannot synthesise them from their individual components. Green plants, however, possess certain pigments, predominantly chlorophyll, which give them precisely this ability. Chlorophyll is quite remarkable in that it makes it possible for green plants (including algae, of course) to combine carbon dioxide and water into carbohydrates in a complicated series of reactions, as long as there is light available. Interestingly, one of the by-products of this process is oxygen which, itself, is absolutely essential for survival. The whole series of reactions is collectively referred to as photosynthesis and can be represented chemically by the equation shown above.

Since photosynthesis is dependent on light, it follows that plants cannot photosynthesise at night. Respiration, however, continues unabated day and night. Whereas photosynthesis uses sunlight energy and carbon dioxide and releases oxygen, the opposite is true of respiration, i.e. it uses up oxygen and releases both carbon dioxide and energy as shown in the second equation (above).

This situation has led to a common misunderstanding which has even found its way into some aquarium books. There are various forms of the misunderstanding, the worst being those that imply that plants photosynthesise during the day and respire at night. The truth of the matter is that plants photosynthesise *only* during the day but respire *all the time*.

During the day, though (particularly if conditions are very favourable), the rate at which photosynthesis proceeds far outstrips that at which respiration takes place. The result is that the plant requires more carbon dioxide at such times that it is capable of generating through respiration. Therefore, it ends up taking in carbon dioxide from the water. This process has sometimes been wrongly referred to as 'breathing' and has, no doubt, contributed to the confusion.

As stated earlier, animals, including fish, cannot synthesise their own carbohydrates. However, they all need carbohydrates in order to survive. Some species, the herbivores, consume plants directly, obtaining their full complement in this fashion. Others will eat the herbivores or other fish which, in turn, feed on the herbivores. Carbohydrates are, therefore, obtained by every species through a similar chain of feeding strategies as that employed in obtaining proteins.

Despite the universal requirements for

carbohydrates, it does not follow that all species of fish require the same amount. Goldfish (*Carassius auratus*), for example, require a diet richer in carbohydrates than a carnivore/piscivore, such as the Jewel Cichlid (*Hemichromis bimaculatus*).

Vitamins Even if a fish's diet is perfectly balanced in terms of proteins, lipids and carbohydrates, serious problems will arise if one or more vitamins are either lacking or present in insufficient quantity. For example, a diet low in Vitamin A can lead to defective vision, while one low in Vitamin D will affect bone formation through the disruption of the processes involved in calcium and phosphorus assimilation. Lack of pyridoxine (Vitamin B_6) will impair both protein and fat metabolism. Carbohydrate metabolism will be likewise affected if there is insufficient riboflavin (Vitamin B_2). Lack of ascorbic acid (Vitamin C) has been shown to be responsible for bent/curved spine deformities (scoliosis) in certain species.

Clearly, then, no diet can afford to be deficient in vitamins for any length of time. Yet, despite their significance, fish only require small amounts of vitamins in their food.

Minerals (Trace Elements) Minerals are also referred to as Trace Elements because they are required in very small amounts by both aquatic animals and plants. Although we know what many of the 25 or so minerals are required for, details of actual, individual amounts are very difficult to estimate. One of the main reasons for this is that aquatic organisms absorb minerals both from the food they consume as well as from the water itself. This last point is very significant in that it illustrates the importance of correct water chemistry. If a species lives in a particular type of water in the wild, this, obviously, means that it has evolved to survive under a particular set of conditions. These conditions include a certain, possibly unique, complement of mineral salts, some of which will be absolutely essential for the continued survival of all the species found in that environment. Two well-known, contrasting examples are the soft, acid, (often) humus-stained waters in which many South American Tetras are found, and the normally clear, hard, alkaline conditions which exist in the African Rift Lakes where Mbuna Cichlids live.

It is quite easy to provide all the mineral salts that aquarium fish need by matching pH and water hardness conditions as recommended for each species and combining them with a balanced diet. Failure to comply with such guidelines can result in a lack of one or more essential trace elements which, in turn, will lead to some deficiency-associated breakdown or disease. For example, lack of calcium and/or phosphorus will inhibit bone formation (among other metabolic processes). At best, fish suffering from such a deficiency will exhibit retarded growth. In extreme cases, so many enzymatic processes may become affected that the fish can die. Iodine is necessary for balanced hormone activity, while iron is essential for oxygen transport, energy transfer and the formation of haemoglobin (the red blood pigment) itself. Even chlorine, which is highly toxic when present in excess, is necessary, along with sodium and potassium.

If an aquarium is maintained efficiently, with adequate plant and fish stocks, an appropriate feeding regime and regular partial water changes, the chances are that there will always be sufficient trace elements present to meet the needs of both fish and plants. If a deficiency is suspected, however, supplements may be added, at least until a more satisfactory balance has been worked out.

Foods and Feeding

The point has been made earlier that the 'aim' of feeding is to provide an adequate supply of all essential nutritional requirements. In the wild, these have to be sought by the fish themselves. The fact that so many species survive and breed in such profusion is proof (if proof were needed) that they manage perfectly well, overall. This is despite the fact that many individuals may die in the process, often falling prey to members of their own species. Yet, as a whole, there exists some form of diet-based equilibrium that plays a major role in maintaining numbers at fairly constant levels. This birth/death cycle could, therefore, be seen as a means of continual distribution of proteins, fats, carbohydrates, vitamins and trace elements. Within the confines of an aquarium, though, this is neither always possible nor, indeed, ever desirable. Simple steps, such as separating incompatible species or adult and young stages, are effective partial solutions. However, having thus deprived the fish of natural sources of food, the aquarist must replace these with efficient substitutes. Nowadays, this is both relatively easy and inexpensive in the majority of cases. If there exists a problem for the new aquarist, it lies in selecting a suitable food from the vast array of commercially produced flakes, pellets, tablets, foodsticks, gamma-irradiated deep-frozen or freeze-dried foods, cultured livefoods and other equally tempting offerings.

Clearly, it would be impractical (in fact, impossible) to deal with every type of food available to aquarists here. However, it is not difficult to provide some general guidelines which can then be adapted accordingly.

Summary of Commercial Foods

Category	Range
Flakes	1. Formulae to suit most fish, i.e. staple diet. 2. Formulae to suit specific types of fish, e.g. vegetable or meat/fish-based diets. 3. Formulae aimed at specific functions, e.g. growth, colour, conditioning and tablet foods (compressed flakes).
Pellets and Foodsticks	1. Formulae to suit a range of fish, i.e. staple diet. 2. Formulae and sizes to suit specific types of fish, e.g. high protein for carnivores, floating for surface feeders and hand feeding.
Fry Foods	1. Dry preparations (powder) for specific types of fry, i.e. egglayer or livebearer fry. 2. Liquid preparations for specific purposes, e.g. suspensions for fry to feed on, or suspensions to stimulate infusoria for the fry to feed on. 3. Brine Shrimp Eggs (*Artemia salina*) – need to be hatched by the aquarist (directions usually provided) and then fed to fry. 4. Infusoria – cultures of microscopic organisms which can be fed directly to fry or cultured and fed on a regular basis.
Freeze-dried Foods	1. Loose – designed for sprinkling on the water surface and best suited to surface feeders: Bloodworms, midge/mosquito larvae and shrimps are the most common varieties. 2. In blocks – designed for pressing on to inside of aquarium; suitable for all types of feeders. Most common varieties are *Tubifex* worms and shrimps.
Gamma-irradiated, Deep-frozen Foods	Fast-expanding range includes *Daphnia*, *Tubifex*, *Mysis*, razor clams, mussels, shrimps, krill, algae, lance fish and plankton. Particles often too large for small fish and delicate feeders (can, however, be ground down to size).

COMMERCIAL FOODS The water content of the food that fish eat in the wild is usually between 70 and 90 per cent. Therefore, in order to obtain sufficient nourishment, fish need to eat relatively large amounts of food. By contrast, many commercial foods, particularly flakes, sticks, pellets and all the freeze-dried varieties, can contain as little as 3 per cent water or less.

If the quality of the nutritional components of these commercial foods matches that found in nature, it follows that a small portion of good-quality manufactured food will be equivalent, in nutritional value, to a much larger amount of naturally available food.

Some manufactured foods actually do come quite close to natural foods in quality, thus making the aquarist's job quite an easy one. Such foods have great advantages in that they can be stored for considerable periods even after opening. They are also clean to handle, take up little shelf space, are relatively inexpensive, are available all the year round and, very importantly, exist in a range of formulae suited virtually to every type of fish likely to be kept in an aquarium. For example, there are vegetable flakes for herbivorous species, meat/fish-based flakes for carnivores/piscivores, growth flakes (with higher protein levels) for young, growing fish, colour flakes with added pigmentation enhancers, conditioning flakes to build up fish in preparation for spawning . . . the list goes on, and these are just the flakes! Tablets, foodsticks and pellets are usually based on formulae derived from one or more of the above. For young fish, there are finely powdered foods, liquid foods, infusoria (microscopic organisms) stimulators, infusoria cultures, plankton suspensions, brine shrimp eggs for hatching and many others.

On the freeze-dried front, a wide range of food organisms are available. Some are loose and can be sprinkled on the surface of the water, while others are compacted into blocks which can be pressed on to the inside of the aquarium where they will stick and from which the fish will quickly learn to feed. The most popular freeze-dried foods are *Tubifex* worms, mosquito/midge larvae, shrimps and bloodworms.

Recent years have seen the introduction of gamma-irradiated frozen foods which are, therefore, free of pathogenic (disease-causing) organisms. One great advantage that these foods possess is that they are often more readily accepted by fish which have rejected other types of food. One disadvantage over other commercial foods, albeit a small one, is that gamma-irradiated foods need to be stored in a freezer. The moisture content of these foods is, of course, as high as that which exists in naturally available foods. The range, which is continually being expanded, includes *Daphnia*, squid, bloodworms, *Mysis* shrimps, razor clams, plankton, prawns, mussels, algae, lance fish, krill and *Tubifex* worms.

LIVEFOODS As their name implies, these foods are fed to the fish alive. Their inclusion with commercial foods, such as flakes and freeze-dried preparations, is justified on the grounds that they are the main 'live' foods which have traditionally been sold over the counter in the same way as any of the dry or prepared foods. This situation is, however, changing in that an ever-increasing variety of other livefoods is being cultured and sold in the same way. Perhaps the best-known of these are the Brine Shrimp Rearing Kits which allow the aquarist to hatch the shrimps and rear them to maturity using the food provided in the kit.

Livefoods have several significant advantages. The one that is most immediately apparent is that they move. This invariably elicits a response in even those species or individuals that are normally reluctant to feed. Therefore, as long as a suitable supply of livefood is available, such fish can be kept in good condition with relative ease.

Aquatic livefoods (as opposed to terrestrial livefoods), particularly those which form part of a fish's natural diet, are likely to contain some of the minerals which are vital either for keeping a fish in a state of good health or, most importantly, for bringing it into breeding condition. It is possible, therefore, that some species which prove rather difficult to spawn in captivity, such as Red Tailed Black Sharks (*Labeo bicolor*) or Clown Loaches (*Botia macracantha*), could be induced to breed regularly if we knew their exact food intake in the wild and could reproduce it in aquaria. Breeding success is not, of course, governed by diet alone, but it may be more significant than it is often given credit for.

On the debit side, it is quite easy for unwanted or potentially dangerous organisms to be introduced into an aquarium in a batch of wild-caught aquatic livefood. For example, small Damselfly and Dragonfly nymphs will grow into large, well-fed predators in an amazingly short time in a tropical aquarium where they can hide, hunt and escape detection among the plants. Both can be easily and inadvertently introduced with wild-caught *Daphnia*, glassworms, bloodworms and mosquito larvae. *Tubifex* worms are normally found in polluted environments and can transfer pathogens into an aquarium unless they are thoroughly cleaned. The aquarist must, therefore, beware and take appropriate measures. The safest way to avoid these problems (other than by avoiding livefoods altogether) is either to culture one's own livefood supply or else use terrestrial instead of aquatic foods. Another drawback with livefoods is that many of them are seasonal, being abundant during the warmer months of the year and virtually disappearing during autumn and winter.

By setting up cultures of various livefoods, the aquarist not only overcomes disease and predator problems but can also ensure a regular supply of, at least, some food organisms all the year round. The range of aquatic livefoods that can be used is very extensive indeed and includes, among many others, *Daphnia*, glassworms, bloodworms, mosquito/midge larvae, infusoria, *Cyclops*, brine shrimps (larvae and adults), fairy shrimps, freshwater shrimps (*Gammarus*), aquatic snails and *Tubifex* worms. The list of terrestrial livefoods is also quite impressive, with whiteworms, grindal worms, micro-worms, earthworms, mealworms and fruitflies being the most popular with aquarists.

CULTURING LIVEFOODS All of the above foods can be cultured with varying degrees of ease and, often, without the need to provide large rearing accommodation. The following information on the culturing of some livefoods is meant as a guide only, not as a definite set of rules. Experimentation and experience will soon provide alternative techniques. However, it is always best to start by following methods that have proved successful for others.

LIVEFOODS FOR JUVENILE AND ADULT FISH
Mosquito and Midge, Gnat Larvae (Including Bloodworms and Glassworms) All of these are immature stages of Dipteran (mosquito-type) insects. Therefore, they represent short-term foods which must be used quickly before they change, or metamorphose, into flying adults. Troughs of water left out in the open during spring and summer often become colonised with the egg rafts and (later) larvae of one or other of these organisms. However, since this is a hit-and-miss affair, it is better to 'seed' a trough with bags of larvae bought at the local petshop or else collected from a colonised pond. If the starter culture is large enough, some adults will mate soon after emerging and are likely to lay their eggs in the same trough in

which they, themselves, completed their development. Once a breeding sequence has been established, it will usually provide an unbroken supply of larvae for at least three months. The only food that needs to be added to that which develops naturally in the water is an occasional sprinkling of powdered or liquid fish fry food.

Daphnia, Cyclops, Fairy Shrimps and Freshwater Shrimps (Gammarus) These small crustaceans are all easy to culture on a diet of fresh yeast/sugar mixture, dried yeast, free-floating algae (green water), liquid or powdered fish fry food, *small* amounts of well-rotted manure, rabbit droppings or a host of other foods. The essential factors are that the food particles be small enough for the animals to consume and the water be pollution-free. Manure and droppings stimulate the growth of microscopic organisms which, in turn, are eaten by the crustaceans. If the troughs, whose surface should measure at least 60x30 cm (24x12 in), are kept outside, the supply of livefood will dwindle during autumn and will virtually disappear during winter. If the

cultures are brought indoors, aerated vigorously and illuminated continuously, they will provide a permanent supply throughout the year.

One great advantage that these livefoods have over many others is that, being truly aquatic for the whole of their lives, they can be left indefinitely in an aquarium without fear of decomposition or of metamorphosis into flying adults.

Tubifex Worms These worms, belonging to the family Tubificidae, generally inhabit mud-flats which are often deficient in oxygen and where, consequently, there are large numbers of anaerobic (non-oxygen-dependent) micro-organisms, including potentially dangerous bacteria. *Tubifex* worms are inexpensive and available all the year round in petshops. They are, therefore, hardly ever cultured. They can, however, be maintained alive for several days without food by standing a shallow dish (where they will form a ball) under a dripping tap. This keeps them relatively clean and reduces the risk of introducing disease into the aquarium. Nevertheless, *Tubifex* worms should always be

Below left: Aerated Brine Shrimp hatching/culture bottle
Below right: Brine Shrimp may be dispensed into the sieve by blowing gently down the short tube

Bottom: Infusoria may be drip-fed to very young fry using this technique based on the siphon principle

Chironomid larvae (Bloodworms) are accepted by most fish

Mysid Shrimps are best collected from brackish water lakes

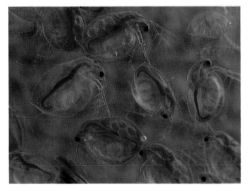

The most common livefood of all is *Daphnia*

Glassworms (*Chaoborus*) can be bought in sachets in some shops

given a good rinse just before they are fed to fish. There are also some sterilising preparations and *Tubifex* feeders available from shops. Both reduce risks still further and the feeders keep the worms confined to a relatively small space making it easy for the fish to find them.

Aquatic Snails Unless precautions are taken, snails will appear sooner or later in most tropical freshwater aquaria where, every so often, they undergo a population explosion. Rather than dispose of them, many aquarists simply collect them, squash them and throw them back into the tank. Most fish, particularly carnivorous species, relish these occasional feasts. If a regular supply of snails is required, then they can be easily cultured in a small tank on a diet of lettuce, squashed or degenerating leaves of aquatic plants, or any of the commercial fish foods.

Adult Brine Shrimp Up to quite recently, these crustaceans (*Artemia salina*) were only popular as newly hatched nauplii larvae used to feed fry (see page 25). However, rearing kits are now available which include food, rearing tank and packets of the salt necessary to make up the culture solution. Alternatively, 20 gm of rock salt per litre of water and a tube of one of the liquid preparations available for feeding to *marine* invertebrates will prove quite satisfac-

tory. Numerous petshops also now sell live adult Brine Shrimp just as they do *Daphnia, Tubifex* and other livefoods. Since these crustaceans live in saltwater, they must be sieved and the water discarded or returned to the rearing vessel before they are fed to the fish. If large numbers are being fed or if the feeds are very regular, a quick rinse under the tap will prevent a gradual build-up of salt.

Whiteworms and Grindal Worms Whiteworms (*Enchytraeus albidus*) and Grindal Worms (*Enchytraeus buchholzi*) are terrestrial Enchytraeids (related to Earthworms) which have long been popular with aquarists. The easiest way to distinguish between them with the naked eye is by their size. *E. albidus* grows much larger attaining a maximum size of around 2 cm, while full-grown *E. buchholzi* are usually about 1 cm in total length.

Culture methods are similar for both, the only significantly different parameter being temperature: around 24°C (75°F) for Grindal Worms and around 20°C (68°F) or less for Whiteworms. A container (wood, glass or plastic) measuring around 30x20x15 cm deep (12x8x6 in) is filled with moist loam or leaf mould to about 2 cm from the top edge. The small initial culture of worms is then placed on top and allowed to disperse. A moist piece of bread, cooked cereal or potato is next pushed gently into the loam to lie more or less flush with the surface. Finally, a small sheet of glass or plastic (just slightly smaller than the size of the container) is laid on the surface of the medium and the culture is stored in a warm place for a few weeks. At the end of this period, there should be enough worms to feed as a regular treat to fish. Exclusive feeding on Whiteworms or Grindal Worms should be avoided because of their high fat content.

Earthworms Earthworms are members of the family Lumbricidae. The two species most frequently used as food for fish are the Common Earthworm (*Lumbricus terrestris*) and the smaller and thinner Long Worm (*Allolobophora longa*). They can be fed whole, chopped or shredded according to circumstances. During the warmer months of the year, provided conditions are humid enough, there is usually a plentiful supply of earthworms in any garden. It is possible to 'encourage' them even during dry spells by laying damp sacking in a shady corner and preventing it from drying out by frequent spraying. During the colder months, it is quite possible to keep the culture going by applying the same principle, i.e. moisture, organic food, such as dead leaves or bran, darkness and reasonable warmth. All that is required is a substantial box, 60 x 30 x 15 cm (24 x 8 x 6 in) filled with good-quality loam and 'seeded' with a stock population of earthworms, dug up undamaged, from the garden. Such a culture may also produce other unintentional food items such as small snails, slugs, woodlice, etc. However, cultures of this type have a tendency to go sour and, when they do, must be discarded and a fresh start made.

Mealworms The name Mealworm is given to the larvae of various beetles, e.g. *Tenebrio molitor*, *T. obscurus*, *Blapstinus moestus* and *Alphitobius diaperinus*. Although the size of the 'worms' varies from species to species, most only grow to a maximum of about 2 cm in length. Culturing these organisms can easily become a fascinating activity in its own right.

Basically, Mealworms require a temperature around 27°c (80°F) and will feed on a wide range of vegetable matter. Suitable easy food items include bran, wholewheat flakes, cornmeal, potatoes and carrots. Incidentally, Mealworms will also chew through cardboard – something that must be borne in mind when choosing suitable accommodation. Plastic and most other types of container can, however, be used as long as ventilation is possible. Crumpled up newspaper

should also be provided to allow the larvae to hide and pupate. The adults emerge approximately three weeks after pupation and start laying eggs within eight days or so. These take about a fortnight to hatch. Therefore, within a few months, quite a thriving colony may be established from just a few larvae.

Fruitflies Fruitflies are known scientifically as *Drosophila*. There are numerous species but one in particular, *D. melanogaster*, has been reared in captivity for many years and is used extensively in genetics research. As a result, countless varieties have been produced, including one known as Wingless or Vestigeal Winged. These mutants are incapable of flying and are, therefore, suitable as floating livefoods.

Culture media can be produced in a variety of ways. By far the simplest method is to use one or other of the instant media available from biological suppliers. Preparation of these media simply involves mixing the required amount of medium and water in a culture bottle (milk bottles are ideal) and then sprinkling a little of the dried yeast provided on the surface. After adding the starter culture (available either by mail via magazine advertisements or direct from biological suppliers) the bottle is loosely stoppered, with cotton wool or a piece of foam, and placed in a warm place. Several days later, a second culture is set up either with the surviving flies, or with a fresh supply, to provide continuity. At 25°c (77°F), the whole cycle from egg to adult can be completed in about 10 days. Since fruitflies are very prolific, a regular and abundant supply can be obtained from just a handful of cultures.

LIVEFOODS FOR FRY
Infusoria This covers a range of organisms whose shared characteristics are that they are microscopic and aquatic. The best known and, consequently, the one most commonly used as a first food for fry is the protozoan (single-celled animal) *Paramecium*, the Slipper Animalcule.

There are various methods of culturing infusoria, the following being the three most popular ones:
1. Lettuce, turnip, hay, potato or banana skins are squashed and/or boiled and added to a jar of aquarium water. After a few days in a warm environment, the water turns cloudy (and smelly!). Individual drops will show a profusion of microscopic organisms which can be fed with a pipette to fry as soon as they consume their embryonic yolk sacs and become free-swimming.

2. There are liquid fry-food preparations available in most shops which can be added directly to the fry rearing tank or to the infusoria culture. If added to the fry tank, some of the liquid food may be eaten directly by the fish themselves. The rest is consumed by the infusoria, consequently, multiply and, in so doing, provide the fry with a regular supply of food.
3. Apple or Mystery Snails (*Ampullaria*) are large aquatic snails with appetites to match. They will eat virtually anything, animal or vegetable, but tend to leave most species of healthy aquatic plants alone, preferring, instead, dead or dying leaves and algae. Their usefulness from the fry rearing point of view is that their faeces contain substances which stimulate the growth of infusoria. The snails can either be introduced into the tank shortly after the fry have hatched or, better still, they can be cultured in a separate tank from which infusoria-rich water can be drawn on a regular basis.

Newly Hatched Brine Shrimp After the first week or so, most fry are too large to exist and grow entirely on a diet of infusoria. For some species, in fact, infusoria are too small from the moment of birth (livebearer fry fall into this category). One of the best alternatives is provided by the newly hatched larvae (nauplii) of *Artemia salina*, the Brine Shrimp. Hatching kits, which include eggs, hatchery, salt and a fine sieve, are universally available. Alternatively, the eggs may be bought and hatched in a wide-necked bottle using a well-aerated solution made up of approximately 20 gm (one teaspoonful) of rock salt in one litre of water. Many brands of table salt contain additives which inhibit hatching. These should, therefore, be avoided.

At a temperature in the region of 25°c (77°F), the eggs will begin to hatch after about a day. The turbulence created by the airstone will, obviously, keep the larvae and their empty egg shells in suspension. However, if the air supply is stopped several minutes before feeding, the shells will float while the larvae will sink. These can then be siphoned into a fine sieve by means of a rubber/plastic tube. The water is returned to the culture bottle and the brine shrimp are given a light rinse in tapwater to remove traces of salt prior to feeding to the fry. It should be remembered that *Artemia* lives in saline conditions and will die in a freshwater aquarium after a few hours. Care must, therefore, be exercised in the amount offered at any one time.

Microworms These small Nematodes (*Anguillula silusiae*) are also variously known as Microeels or Eelworms. They are even smaller than Whiteworms or Grindal Worms (see p. 23) and are suitable for feeding to the fry of egglayers which are very small at birth, e.g. most Gouramis, once they are about two weeks old. Large egglayer fry, such as those of many Cichlids, and livebearer fry can usually take Microworms as soon as they have absorbed their yolk sacs.

The culture medium consists of moist oatmeal in a shallow container (a medium-sized plastic flower pot saucer is ideal). The culture of Microworms is simply mixed in with the medium, covered by a sheet of glass or plastic and left in a warm place (*c*. 25°c/77°F). The worms multiply very quickly and will climb up the sides of the container, remaining just above the culture medium. They are then removed with a small brush and fed directly to the fish. Since oatmeal goes sour after a short time, the best way to avoid problems (and foul smell) is to start a series of cultures every few days and discard old ones every 10 days or so.

The Importance of Correct Feeding

The moment fish are introduced into an aquarium, they forfeit most of their freedom in terms of the range and amount of food they can consume. Therefore, it is the duty of every aquarist to ensure that each fish receives sufficient food of the appropriate type and quality. This can be done very easily in the vast majority of cases. All it takes is a little thought and commonsense. In this way, many distressing and potentially dangerous situations can be avoided. For example, slow-moving, nocturnal and bottom-living species will invariably lose out if the feeding technique adopted by the aquarist is suited to fast-moving, diurnal (active during the day), surface and midwater feeders. Fish most often at the losing end of such arrangements are those usually referred to as 'scavengers'. These include many species of Catfish and bottom-living Loaches, such as the various Kuhlies or Coolies (*Acanthophthalmus* spp). A common mistake is to regard these fish as capable of surviving on the leftovers of the other tank inhabitants. This is, of course, quite wrong. All it takes to avoid problems is the pre-soaking of some of the food, if it is a dry preparation, in order to make it sink quickly to the bottom (introducing flakes edge-on into the water has a similar effect), placing a food tablet or freeze-dried block strategically close to the bottom, adding a small second feed after the surface swimmers have had their fill, or any other strategy that will ensure that an adequate amount of food reaches these fish.

In the case of algae eaters, such as the Sucking Loach (*Gyrinocheilus aymonieri*), it is quite pointless treating the tank with an algicide to get rid of encrusting algae from the rocks and sides of the aquarium and expect this species to do well without a vegetable component to the diet.

It is, therefore, imperative to find out as much as one can about the dietary requirements and feeding habits of each fish at the very outset.

Establishing the Correct Amounts of Food Required

Having established a fish's requirements, it is equally important to supply the correct amount of food. Fish often 'appear hungry' and will come to the front of the aquarium as soon as anyone approaches. This does not, however, mean that they are underfed. The opposite is more likely to be true. Excess food will suffer one of two possible fates:

1. It may be consumed, usually rather slowly, but, being surplus to requirements, may be laid down as unrequired and potentially dangerous fat deposits around the internal organs. This type of activity is also associated with excessive production of nitrogen-rich toxic waste products which can quickly lead to serious chemical imbalance in the water (see page 27).
2. Some or all of the excess may remain uneaten and will soon begin to degenerate. In so doing, it will deplete the oxygen level of the water and will lead to the production of toxic substances, often accompanied by a characteristic foul smell and black patches on the gravel around the rotting bits of food. The implications of this situation are obvious.

Overfeeding must, therefore, be avoided at all costs. The problem, though, is establishing what *is* enough. By far the best way of doing this is to start by intentionally attempting to *underfeed*. If the amount is too little or just enough, it will be completely consumed within a few minutes. If there is any food after, say, ten minutes, then this can be taken as an unequivocal sign that overfeeding has taken place. Trial and error will soon put the aquarist right. If overfeeding has taken place, then all the food left over must be removed to prevent it from rotting and polluting the aquarium water.

Once the correct amount has been established, then several small feeds can be supplied every day, the frequency depending on a number of factors, like the type of species (carnivores tend to eat fewer, larger feeds than herbivores or omnivores) or the age of the fish (young, growing fish tend to prefer more frequent feeds than adult or old specimens).

A good way of avoiding overfeeding is to follow what could be termed 'The Five-Minute Rule'. According to this, *the correct amount of food is that which will be completely consumed within five minutes.*

Long-term and Vacation Feeding Programmes

On the whole, aquarium fish get all the food they need and a little more besides. Many experienced aquarists have a weekly feeding programme of six days feeding/one day fast. This seems to suit most species and individuals, except growing juveniles and adults being conditioned for spawning.

During the day of fast, the fish use up a little of their excess fat reserves and can obtain a small amount of food from any items of nutritional value that may be present in the tank, such as algae, small snails, etc.

If the feeding programme is well-balanced in terms of amount and quality, then fish can be left unfed for several weeks. This makes them ideal pets in terms of holiday care. Unless one's neighbour is a fishkeeper or can be trained to feed correct amounts, tropical freshwater fish are best left unfed at such times. It does not seem to bother them unduly and they often look sleeker and more alert after an enforced break.

Alternatively, there are 'weekend blocks' and 'holiday blocks' available which supply small amounts of food in a slowly soluble matrix. These can be left in the aquarium and will allow the fish to obtain some food over a period of time. However, as the matrix dissolves, it will cause an increase in harness and pH with the result that the water will become more alkaline. A partial water change should, therefore, be carried out on returning home after a break. A holiday feeding programme of preselected types and amounts of food can also be carried out by means of an automatic feeder. There are some very sophisticated models available nowadays which will set the mind of even the most concerned aquarist at rest. Even if you fall within the 'best-left-unfed' category, these feeders are well worth considering, particularly if you have a tankful of young, growing fish at the time.

Fish Health

A healthy fish is a joy to watch, while an unhealthy one is, at best, distressing to witness. Since it would be naive to believe that all one's fish will remain healthy all the time, there will, inevitably, be some periods of distress.

Much of the real art of fish keeping is, therefore, concerned with the enjoyable side of the hobby. Despite the gloomy, depressing feelings that detailed accounts of fish diseases invariably elicit, the truth of the matter is that the vast majority of serious problems can be avoided. The main ingredient of this formula is a sound understanding of the reasons why fish succumb to disease. Such an appreciation enhances the fishes' chances of experiencing good health and, consequently, contributes significantly to our own enjoyment at seeing them healthy.

The secret of success starts, quite naturally, with the water itself. It is one of the three main factors responsible for the state of health of a fish. The other two are the fish themselves and the pathogenic (disease-causing) organisms which are always present in the water. As long as all three are in equilibrium, the fish stand a good chance of remaining healthy. However, alter any of the three (for example, by lowering the fishes' resistance through improper feeding) and problems will arise.

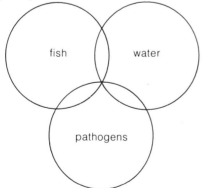

The fish and their environment need to be in harmony

The Significance of Good Water

No one doubts the importance of pollution-free air in maintaining the health of terrestrial organisms. If the same awareness were to be applied to aquatic organisms, then fewer fish would succumb to disease. It is an inescapable fact that poor water quality results in poor quality fish. The logic of this statement is almost self-evident. Yet the establishment and maintenance of good water quality is often relegated way down the list of priorities. Part of the reason for this is that water can often be well below the standards required by fish but look as if it were in perfect condition. Therefore, while most people will recognise an extreme case of poor water quality by its characteristic odour or turbidity, or by the abnormal behaviour of the fish themselves, less severe cases can escape detection until it is too late. This is because many toxic substances are soluble and, consequently, invisible to the naked eye.

Problems Associated with Water Quality

Chlorine and Chloramine Chlorine and, more recently, chloramine are additives designed to render tapwater fit for drinking. 'Drinking' is the operative word here; tapwater was never designed specifically for fishkeeping – at least, not the way it comes out of the tap. Both chlorine and chloramine are toxic to fish and, obviously, have to be eliminated.

The elimination of chlorine presents no real problems. There are efficient dechlorinators available commercially which are capable of neutralising chlorine quickly and safely. Even in the absence of these water treatments, chlorine will dissipate of its own accord within 24 hours or so, particularly if the water is aerated vigorously.

Chloramine presents a somewhat different picture. Dechlorinators will help to break it down to an extent. Unfortunately, one of the by-products of this process is ammonia which, as has been mentioned elsewhere is highly toxic. In an aquarium with an efficient biological filter, the ammonia will be converted into nitrites and, finally, nitrates. In new aquaria, this is, clearly, not possible, bearing in mind that it can take up to six months for a biological filter to become fully functional. In such cases, alternative methods of removing the ammonia need to be installed. Compounds such as activated charcoal and zeolite will do the job quite effectively and can be incorporated as part of a power filter sandwich. In fact, even established biological filters can do with a little bit of help during major water changes.

Aeration is not much use in getting rid of chloramine because it takes about one week of uninterrupted vigorous ventilation to complete the job. The fish, of course, cannot wait that long!

Metallic Ions/Salts Aquatic organisms are very susceptible to metal poisoning. Although this problem was more prevalent in the past when aquaria with exposed angle iron frames were regularly used, it is still quite possible to introduce poisonous metal compounds into aquaria if no thought is given to the subject.

The main source of this type of poisoning is water drawn early in the morning from metal pipes in which there has been a gradual build-up of these chemicals overnight. The solution could not be simpler; all one need do is run the tap for several minutes before drawing any water destined for an aquarium. The most common metals implicated in poisoning are copper, zinc, lead and iron, the last of which (in particular) is actually required in minute quantities by plants for healthy growth.

To be on the safe side, newly drawn water should be treated with a tapwater conditioner which will prevent most of the potentially toxic effects of metals. Fish suffering from metal poisoning exhibit an acceleration of the respiratory rate (as observed by the movement of the gill covers) during the early stages followed by gasping at the surface, even in well-oxygenated water. Close examination of the gill filaments will show them to be inflamed, damaged and clumped together. In severe cases, this will lead to death through suffocation. In less severe cases, the considerable stress that this condition produces will lower the fishes' resistance to other diseases. A check on the levels of some of the metals present in water can be kept quite easily by means of a suitable water testing kit.

Ammonia The production of ammonia by aquatic organisms and chloramine breakdown has already been discussed. However, there are other potential sources of this highly poisonous chemical, such as fumes from certain industrial processes or (more commonly) from household ammonia-based cleaning compounds. Whatever the source, the results are the same, with symptoms not unlike those produced by metal poisoning. The actual toxicity of ammonia is affected by the pH (acidity/alkalinity) of the water. For example, if the water is neutral or slightly acid, very little ammonia remains in the toxic un-ionised form for long. However, as the pH moves into the alkaline part of the scale, this percentage rises quite dramatically. Viewed in this way, the use of ammonia-absorbing media, such as zeolite or activated carbon, adopts a progressively more vital role the higher the pH of the water becomes. Ammonia and the nitrites that it can be converted into may both be measured with an inexpensive testing kit.

Oxygen and Nitrogen If the oxygen concentration of the water is too low (the required level may vary for particular species) this will lead to a number of complications, such as reduced ability to respire, loss of colour and general overall condition, loss of appetite, increased susceptibility to infections, and so on.

If, however, the amount of oxygen and nitrogen dissolved in the water is very high, this will cause the fishes' blood to become supersaturated with these gases. As long as the status quo is maintained, the fish will be all right. If, however, there is a sharp drop in the oxygen concentration of the water, such as that produced in a heavily planted tank after the lights are switched off, the excess pressure of gases present in the blood will cause the formation of tiny bubbles under the skin, in the fins and, particularly, around the head and eyes. In serious cases, the eye may be pushed partly out of its socket, giving rise to a condition known as Exophthalmia, Exophthalmus or Pop-eye. Abrupt gas imbalances can also be caused when a major water change is carried out involving the replacement of well-oxygenated aquarium water with poorly oxygenated tapwater. In either case, Gas Bubble Disease (as this complaint is known) is the direct consequence of a badly managed water quality programme and often results in the death of affected fish through embolisms (blockages) of blood vessels.

Extremes in pH Although the majority of fish can live quite happily in water marginally on either side of neutral, i.e. between pH 6.5 and 7.5, some have evolved very specific requirements. These should be checked beforehand to ensure that the water provided is neither too acid nor too alkaline.

If the pH is allowed to drop excessively, say

below 5.5, the water will be too acid for many species. As a result, the fish will suffer from Acidosis. Symptoms may vary but the end-result will not if the situation remains unrectified. The two extremes, in terms of symptoms, are:

1. extremely fast swimming movements, gasping at the surface and occasional jumps out of the water;
2. extreme sluggishness, with a tendency to hide, loss of colour and appetite. In the first case, death is usually quick; in the latter, death is invariably slow.

At the other end of the scale, excessive alkalinity, i.e. pH values above 8.5, can lead to Alkalosis in many species. Serious damage of the gill filaments, a general 'opaqueness' of the skin and disintegration of the fin edges are all associated with this condition. The last of these symptoms must not be confused with Fin Rot which can affect fish at normal pH values. Aquaria which are most likely to develop excessively high pH conditions are those in which the water is soft (thus having little buffering capacity), the plant growth over-abundant and the location one which exposes the tank to too much sunlight.

The pH of an aquarium is easy to measure with an appropriate kit which should, therefore, be considered a must by every aquarist. Regular checks should prevent major fluctuations. If any changes in pH become necessary, these must be carried out gradually. It is not always the poor quality of the water that kills – often it is the abruptness of the change.

Fumes and Sprays It is quite easy to overlook the fact that airborne molecules of toxic substances can dissolve into an aquarium, particularly one having efficient aeration. The results, though, can be quite disastrous. It has not been unknown, for example, for the proud owner of a sophisticated, expensive, wood-panelled aquarium to spray the wood with a furniture polish and then wonder why the fish begin to exhibit signs of distress! Insect sprays, paint fumes, air fresheners and other household aerosols and cleaners are all potentially hazardous to fish. Should water contamination from one of these sources be suspected, an immediate partial water change should be carried out.

Temperature Fluctuations The examples quoted above all show how the chemical quality of the water can affect the health of fish. Temperature is about the only physical parameter whose influence is of the same magnitude. Yet, its effects are often indirect. Tropical fish have evolved to survive at tropical temperatures. Their metabolic reactions are, therefore, finely tuned to these conditions, with each set of enzymes functioning at its best within a relatively narrow temperature range. While a few species, such as the Paradise Fish (*Macropodus opercularis*), can adapt to temperatures well below the normal tropical range, most other species cannot.

As soon as the temperature falls below or rises above the optimum range for a particular species, the level of efficiency of its enzymes and (consequently) the metabolic reactions which they control begin to decrease. Within a short time, there will be a breakdown in one or other vital process which will, obviously, place the fish under stress. If the adverse conditions deteriorate further, total breakdown, i.e.

Pop-eye, or Exophthalmia, is quite common and can originate in several ways

This Platy is suffering from Fin Rot, a disease caused by *Flexibacter columnaris* and (possibly) other bacteria

death, will result. If conditions are rectified in time, relatively minor damage may occur, such as a break-out of White Spot (see page 40–1) in cases of mild chilling.

Symptoms of overheating include initial intensification of coloration, short, sharp, fast bursts of activity, increased rate of respiration and gasping at the surface. Symptoms of chilling may include shimmying (pronounced side-to-side 'wagging' of the body), gradual slowing down, ending up with barely visible gill, fin and body movements, some loss of coloration and periodic or permanent resting on the bottom of the aquarium.

Summary of Ailments Caused by Adverse Environmental (Water Quality) Conditions

Causative Agent	Some Symptoms	Some Preventative Steps and Remedies
Chlorine	Restless movements; loss of balance	Use dechlorinators or vigorously aerate water for 24 hours before use
Chloramine and Ammonia	Inflamed gills and fin edges; blood spots; loss of balance	Use dechlorinators accompanied by ammonia-absorbing medium such as zeolite or activated charcoal
Metallic Ions	Inflamed, clumped gill filaments; accelerated respiratory movements; gasping at surface	Allow tap to run for several minutes before water is drawn for an aquarium. Use tapwater conditioners. Carry out immediate partial water change if poisoning is suspected
Oxygen and Nitrogen	(i) *Excess:* Gas Bubble Disease – small bubbles visible under skin, in fins and around head and eyes; Exophthalmia (Pop-eye)	(i) Locate tank away from direct sunlight if over-stocked with plants. Avoid sudden cutting off of light in well-oxygenated, well-planted tanks. Avoid major changes/replacement of well-aerated aquarium water with poorly oxygenated tapwater
	(ii) *Insufficient oxygen:* Gasping at surface; some loss of colour	(ii) Initiate vigorous aeration. Carry out partial water change
pH	(i) *Acidosis:* (a) Fast swimming movements; gasping at surface; occasional jumps out of the water; *or* (b) Extreme sluggishness; tendency to hide; loss of colour and appetite	(i) Avoid overstocking with fish and understocking with plants. Carry out immediate partial water change. Add appropriate proprietary pH adjuster
	(ii) *Alkalosis:* Serious damage to gills; disintegration of fin edges; general 'opaqueness' of skin	(ii) Locate heavily planted tanks away from prolonged, direct sunlight. Carry out immediate partial water change. Add appropriate proprietary pH adjuster
Fumes and Sprays	Generally as for metallic ions	Carry out immediate partial water change. Ventilate room. Switch off aeration until level of fumes has subsided
Temperature	(i) *Low:* Shimmying; sluggish movements; resting on bottom; reduced gill cover, fin and body movements; some loss of coloration	(i) Check heater and thermostat. Increase temperature gradually by replacing amounts of aquarium water with warmer water in a series of small water changes. Switch on heater/stat
	(ii) *High:* Initial intensification of coloration; increased level of activity (above normal); increased rate or respiration; gasping at surface.	(ii) Check heater and thermostat. Switch off heater/stat until temperature has gradually dropped to required level. Carry out a series of small water changes to reduce temperature slowly.

Problems Associated with Inadequate Nutrition

Balanced Diet and Proper Feeding Although the significance of an adequate diet has already been discussed (see page 16) it is important to stress the value of a suitable diet in terms of the overall health of a fish. As long as a fish receives a well-balanced diet, it will be able (within reason) to withstand attack from pathogenic organisms. However, one may be providing highly nutritious food but be presen-

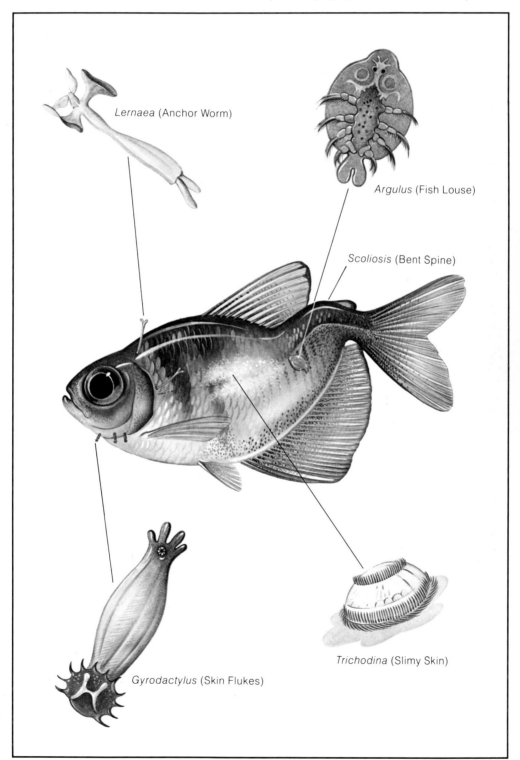

Lernaea (Anchor Worm)

Argulus (Fish Louse)

Scoliosis (Bent Spine)

Trichodina (Slimy Skin)

Gyrodactylus (Skin Flukes)

ting it wrongly, purely in ignorance of the biological characteristics of a particular species. Normally, food should be presented in several portions per day, rather than as a single large feed. The validity of this statement is best illustrated by an example.

Many species of tropical fish belong to the family Cyprinidae. Among these are popular species such as Harlequins (*Rasbora heteromorpha*), Barbs (*Barbus* spp) 'Sharks' (*Labeo* spp) and Danios (e.g. *Brachydanio rerio*, the Zebra). One of the many characteristics that they all share is, somewhat surprisingly, the total lack of a stomach. A biological consequence of this is that Cyprinids are unable to absorb large amounts of nutrients via the gut wall in a single feed (the figure is estimated at around 1 per cent of the total body weight). Yet, these fish need to eat between 2 and 3 per cent of their body weight each day. It is, therefore, pointless to supply Cyprinids with one large feed a day and expect them to grow and enjoy good health. It is far better to present them with their daily requirements in a series of regularly spaced out small feeds.

Proteins The importance of proteins in connection with health is beyond doubt. Without them, tissues cannot be repaired, growth cannot take place, digestion becomes an impossibility and death inevitably will result. Despite this, it is essential to keep things in perspective when choosing a diet for one's fish. Young fish, for example, require higher levels of protein in their food than mature or old individuals. Proteins derived from an animal source are easier to digest than those derived from plants. Evolution has, not surprisingly, resulted in herbivorous species with long alimentary canals and carnivorous/piscivorous ones with correspondingly shorter guts. It does not, therefore, make good sense to choose a vegetable-based flake and feed it to all types of fish. If this is done (or the complete reverse for that matter), dietary problems are likely to develop which will, obviously, reduce the fishes' resistance to all sorts of pathogenic organisms.

With respect to the amount of protein offered, again, it is pointless supplying adult fish with high levels as if they were still growing quickly. In fact if this is done, some of the excess will be expelled as nitrogen-rich, toxic waste products, such as ammonia. Growing fish generally require a diet containing around 35 per cent protein, while fully grown individuals need receive no more than 30 per cent. To provide the latter with any more than this can prove both wasteful and potentially

dangerous. Equally dangerous is a diet which is too low in protein. This results in growth retardation (through lack of 'building materials'), decreased ability to repair tissues and increased susceptibility to infection. Even if the protein level is adequate for normal growth and repair, these processes will prove impossible if other nutrients necessary for energy production, i.e. carbohydrates and fats, are lacking. In such cases, some proteins will be diverted from their primary functions to the generation of energy.

Fats and Oils (Lipids) Although fat is required as a major source of energy, excessive quantities will seriously affect the health of fish in ways similar to those that apply to humans.

Fish swim less in aquaria than in the wild. As a result, they cannot efficiently burn up any excess fat that they may be carrying. This will gradually build up around the internal organs, impairing their ability to function. For example, Carp (*Cyprinus carpio*) kept in captivity have been found to carry between 10 and 45 times more abdominal fat than wild-caught (control) specimens. As fat progressively infiltrates the liver, kidneys, heart and gonads (sexual organs), the affected fish will begin to lose some of its resistance to infection and will gradually be unable to carry out certain vital bodily processes. One such process is the production of gametes (sperm and eggs). Overfat fish are, therefore, next to useless in terms of breeding potential. Excessive fat infiltration of the liver may develop to such an extent that all its filtering and balancing properties may be lost. Fish affected in this way invariably die.

Fat-rich and fat-generating diets must, therefore, be very carefully monitored if their harmful effects are to be avoided. Young fish, fortunately, are not prone to fat-related ailments because they use up large amounts of energy in growth. Little if any fat is, consequently, laid down in store. As a fish matures, though, its growth rate slows down significantly and it is at that stage that an appropriate change in diet becomes essential. This is why fat-rich foods, such as Whiteworms (*Enchytraeus albidus*), are better for growing fish than for adults, and why this livefood is usually recommended as an occasional treat rather than as part of a staple diet.

Carbohydrates Fish metabolism is complex and flexible, making it possible for the same intermediate and/or end-products to be generated in a variety of ways. For example, all fish require carbohydrates, yet some species consume little if any directly. This is particularly so of carnivorous/piscivorous species which, by definition, do not eat plants and are, therefore, denied the most direct method of carbohydrate assimilation. However, the fish they eat will have some carbohydrates present in their tissues, including a store of carbohydrate in the form of glycogen. Large though this amount may be, it may well not provide enough carbohydrate for all the carnivores' metabolic needs. The extra supply comes from a rather unlikely source – protein. As proteins are digested, they are broken down into their constituent amino acids and it is from these that carbohydrates can be synthesised.

This chain reaction shows how interlinked various components of a healthy diet are. It allows us, for example, to see how important a supply of good-quality protein can be in the metabolism of carbohydrates. Another interesting link exists between carbohydrates and fats. As already mentioned, carbohydrates are stored in tissues in the form of glycogen. There is, obviously, a limit to how much glycogen can be stored and, in some cases of excess, carbohydrates will be converted to fats instead. When this happens in fish that are already receiving ample supplies of fats, problems will develop. To make matters worse, fatty degeneration of the liver and other fat-associated diseases can lead to a total disappearance of a fish's store of carbohydrate (glycogen).

Vitamins A well-balanced diet will contain all the vitamins that a fish is likely to require for its everyday needs. If, however, one or more essential ones are missing and this situation is maintained even for a short time, then certain metabolic reactions will be blocked or affected. As a result, the fish will soon begin to show the deficiency symptoms characteristic for the missing vitamin.

Since vitamins perform such a wide range of functions, some of which overlap considerably, it is very difficult to present a complete picture of all their effects. However, as a guide, some of the main functions of 17 vitamins are presented below. It will be seen from the table that many of the reactions influenced by vitamins are fundamental to growth, tissue repair, respiration and other vital metabolic processes, thus underlining their central role in health and survival.

Vitamins	Some Metabolic Processes Affected	Vitamins	Some Metabolic Processes Affected
A	Formation of visual and other pigment; protein metabolism		also found in bone and scales, hence its connection with Scoliosis – Bent Spine)
B₁ (Thiamine)	Oxidation of sugars; proper functioning of nervous system	Choline	Efficient functioning of the nervous system
B₂ (Riboflavin)	Oxidation and respiratory reactions; essential in carbohydrate, fat and protein metabolism	D	Absorption of calcium and phosphorus from the intestine
B₃ (Pantothenic Acid)	Energy release/transformation; balanced functioning of nervous system.	E	Oxidation and respiratory reactions
		Folic Acid	Production of yellow pigments; oxidation and respiratory reactions; glucose regulation
B₆ (Pyridoxine)	Fat and protein metabolism	Inositol	Formation of cell membranes
B₁₂ (Cyanocobalamin)	Protein metabolism; formation of red blood corpuscles (cells) and nucleic acids (found in nuclei, including carriers of genetic information)	K	Formation of blood clotting factors
		Lipoic Acid	Energy release/transformation
Biotin	Fat metabolism	P (Nicotinic Acid or Niacin)	Oxidation and respiratory reactions
C (Ascorbic Acid)	Oxidation and respiratory processes; tissue repair; collagen synthesis (white connective tissue fibres –	Pyridoxal Phosphate	Involved in complex reactions linking proteins with carbohydrates and fats

Minerals (Trace Elements) Mineral salts, while only required in small amounts, are nevertheless just as important in maintaining a fish in a state of good health as any other dietary component. Since some of the 25 or so trace elements which have been shown to be essential can be obtained directly from the water, matching a species with its appropriate water chemistry is very important. If this proves impossible, essential trace elements can also be supplied by means of a balanced diet, such as that provided by today's high-quality commercial foods.

Interestingly, fish appear to use trace elements in a very similar fashion to humans. This can be seen quite clearly in the accompanying table which also demonstrates how critical individual elements can be to the survival of an individual. For example, if the diet is deficient in sulphur, protein synthesis will be badly affected, even if all the other essentials are present in abundance. Lack of iron will affect haemoglobin production which, in turn, will affect the amount of dissolved oxygen that can be carried in the blood.

Minerals	Some Metabolic Processes Affected
Calcium, Fluorine, Magnesium	Bone formation
Phosphorus, Silicon, Chlorine, Potassium, Sodium	Osmoregulation (water balance)
Iron, Sodium	Blood
Calcium, Cobalt, Copper, Iron, Manganese, Molybdenum, Zinc	Formation and action of enzymes
Iodine, Tin	Formation and action of hormones
Potassium	Nerve action
Iron, Phosphorus, Zinc	Energy transfer
Sulphur	Incorporated into proteins and vitamins

Problems Caused by Pathogenic (Disease-causing) Organisms

The problems discussed so far can all be controlled or avoided quite easily. It is true to say that, as long as water quality and diet receive the attention they warrant, few, if any, of the complaints described in connection with these two aspects of fishkeeping will arise. However, there is a third major group of disease-causing agents (pathogenic organisms), which are impossible to avoid completely and, in some instances, may prove difficult to eradicate once established.

Types of Pathogenic Organisms

There are three main types of pathogenic organisms: viruses, bacteria and parasites. One or more of these will, almost invariably, be present in every aquarium. However, if the fish are strong and well-fed and water conditions are good, the chances are that most will be able to resist infection. On the other hand, unfavourable conditions or weakened fish will almost certainly result in an outbreak of disease. The first fish to succumb will be either the weakest individuals which may already be under stress anyway, e.g. by being at the bottom of the pecking order, or those which belong to a species that is particularly susceptible to infection by the pathogen present. Neons (*Paracheirodon innesi*), for example, are more sensitive to attacks from *Plistophora hyphessobryconis*, the protozoan (single-celled organism) which causes Neon Disease, than most other species.

Although there are few viruses which are of any real relevance in terms of causing diseases among aquarium fish, the number of bacterial and parasitic species is much higher. This, coupled with the diversity of life cycles exhibited by parasites, makes the study of fish diseases both a fascinating and highly specialised activity. Diagnosis is not always easy and treatment is sometimes outside the scope of most aquarists. Therefore, whenever there is some doubt, expert advice should be sought from a veterinary surgeon before any treatment is attempted. Further, the use of certain remedies, such as antibiotics, is illegal in some countries unless covered by a vet's prescription. Such details should, of course, be checked thoroughly.

VIRUSES are minute particles, often measuring less than 1 micron (one-thousandth of a millimetre or one millionth of a metre). Most are considerably smaller than bacteria with which they are sometimes wrongly lumped together despite the fact that they are very different indeed.

I have used the word 'particles' to distinguish viruses from living organisms since there is still some doubt in certain quarters concerning their true nature. This doubt arises from the fact that viruses can exist, virtually indefinitely, in crystalline form. When such a crystal encounters a suitable environment, i.e.

Virus Infections

Symptoms	Disease
Hard, whitish or cream-coloured, waxy-like patches which may merge to cover substantial areas of the body.	Pox
Large cauliflower-like growths (sometimes referred to as tumours) or small, isolated, pearl-shaped nodules or warts, caused by enlargement of affected cells by as much as 100,000 times their normal size, distributed on fins or body.	Lymphocystis
Persistent whirling motion along a vertical axis (head-over-heels) or a horizontal one (tail-chasing). May be accompanied by Exophthalmia (Pop-eye) which will not be corrected quickly by improved water conditions.	Whirling Disease. (There is another 'Whirling Disease' caused by a protozoan – see Parasites on page 39).

Fish Pox is caused by a virus but is usually non-fatal

a living organism, it dissolves and releases the numerous individual viruses it contains into the surrounding tissues. These viruses will then invade host cells and release their genetic contents which will become attached to the cell's own genetic material. The infected cell will thus be fooled into producing replicas of the invading viruses. Since replication can take as little as 30 minutes, a virus infection can spread very quickly indeed.

In some cases, affected cells are made to burst, releasing a mass of viruses, each of which can invade another cell. Other viruses can stimulate affected cells to enlarge, giving rise to tumour-like growths. At the moment, viral infections cannot be treated effectively.

Fortunately, only two, Pox and Lymphocystis (possibly three – Whirling Disease), occur in aquaria with any regularity and even these cannot be considered common. Although no treatments are available, symptoms often disappear spontaneously.

BACTERIA are microscopic organisms characterised by, among other things, the absence of a true nucleus enclosed in a nuclear membrane. They are known as Prokaryotes – most organisms, including fish and humans, possess distinct, membrane-bound nuclei and are known as Eukaryotes.

Although many bacteria can cause disease, others are highly beneficial. For example, some bacteria which live inside the alimentary canal of animals help break down the indigestible cellulose walls of plant cells, thus allowing the animals' digestive enzymes access to the nutritional plant cell contents. Other bacteria have already been mentioned (see page 17) in connection with the fixation of atmospheric nitrogen, its assimilation into usable compounds, and the conversion of ammonia to less toxic nitrites and relatively harmless nitrates. In some deep-sea fish, luminescent bacteria can be carried in cheek pouches and are 'switched on or off' at will, by means of tissue covers, to illuminate the way and communicate between members of a shoal. Despite these and other beneficial roles, bacteria can wreak havoc in an aquarium. Fish may die without any apparent symptoms or else may exhibit very distinctive signs of particular bacterial diseases.

If a disease cannot be linked to an environmental, nutritional, viral or parasitic cause, it will almost certainly be the result of a bacterial infection. Bacteria can cause primary infections by direct attack on one or more tissues, or secondary infections by attacking tissues which have already been damaged in some other way, e.g. torn fins, missing scales, body injuries, etc. Woolly growths around the mouth, red sores, ulcers, haemorrhages, rotting fins (or body tissues), extreme sluggishness, recurring loss of scales, general loss of condition and emaciation are all typical symptoms of bacterial disease. Post-mortem examinations carried out by specialists will usually provide a precise diagnosis, provided adequate preservation procedures have been followed. Anyone wishing to make use of these services should first contact the specialists concerned to obtain instructions on the preparation, preservation and packaging of specimens.

Antibiotics, such as chlortetracycline, aureomycin, oxytetracycline, terramycin,

This bacterial infection is aptly named Hole-in-the-Body

The characteristic pine-cone effect caused by Dropsy

chloramphenicol and chloromycetin have all been successfully used in the treatment of bacterial diseases. However, prescriptions are required in certain countries so this must be checked beforehand. I must stress that even these antibiotics may not prove effective if the infection has progressed too far. In such cases, it is far kinder to destroy the affected fish. Gruesome though this may sound, it may well be the only solution but even if the fish is beyond help, its welfare must remain uppermost in the aquarist's mind. Cruelty is unjustifiable at any time. Therefore, on no account must a badly affected dying fish be flushed away out of sight down the toilet. Although this will ultimately kill the fish, it will cause unnecessary, prolonged suffering which the conscientious, caring aquarist cannot allow.

It is far better, however unpleasant or distressing it may be, to destroy the fish quickly either by placing it in a polythene bag and crushing it with a heavy object or by dropping the fish into boiling water. In either case, death is virtually instantaneous. If you are fortunate enough to have a fish anaesthetic at your disposal, you can dispose of your fish quite peacefully by slightly overdosing them.

Antibiotics must be used with great care. An overdose may well kill off the bacteria but it may also cause the death of the fish being treated. Underdosing will leave some bacteria untouched and may lead to the development of a resistant strain. In addition, antibiotics do not normally distinguish between beneficial and pathogenic bacteria and can soon lead to the destruction of an aquarium's established filtering community.

Fortunately, other treatments, besides antibiotics, can also be used on bacterial infections. Their degree of success is variable but, in some cases, they do produce a cure and may well be the only avenue open in certain countries. Compounds which fall into this category are Copper Sulphate, Phenoxethol, Acriflavine and Malachite Green. Directions must be followed closely and overdosing must, again, be avoided. Phenoxethol will maintain

its viability for some time but the other compounds will deteriorate very quickly, often within days. Repeated treatments may, therefore, be necessary. If so, this should be stated clearly on the packaging or enclosed literature.

Antibiotics can have an undesirable side-effect on an aquarium in that some will stimulate the production of aromatic organic compounds which may be detected by their sweet smell. Often, a clouding of the water also occurs, similar in appearance to that observed in new aquaria during the first week or so following setting up. A partial water change carried out after about three days (or sooner if circumstances dictate) should eliminate this problem.

As can be seen from the bacterial disease diagnosis/treatment chart, a particular bacterium can produce a number of symptoms. In addition, similar symptoms may be caused by different bacterial species. Diagnosis is, therefore, not always easy or possible unless specialised testing equipment or expertise is available.

In spite of this, it is usually possible to identify a disease as being bacterial in origin (as opposed to viral or parasitic). If this proves to be the case, a broad-spectrum antibiotic may produce results. If a vet's prescription, with its inevitable expense, is necessary and the infection is acute, it may be wiser to attempt non-antibiotic treatment before proceeding further. Antibiotics must not be seen as the answer to all problems – they are not, and can, when mismanaged, cause more problems than they solve.

If it becomes necessary to destroy all the fish and make a fresh start, all plants must be discarded for fear of re-contamination later. The equipment and gravel must be disinfected either with a proprietary aquarium disinfectant or other suitable solution such as 1–2 per cent formalin. Everything must then be rinsed thoroughly and the gravel examined carefully to remove any dead snails which would otherwise rot, pollute the water and cause yet another series of problems.

Bacterial Infections

Symptoms	Disease	Causative Agents	Some Treatments*
Localised or more general attack on body or fins leading to ulcers or shredding of fin rays. Blood streaks in fin rays usually develop	Fin, Tail or Body Rot (Columnaris Disease)	*Flexibacter columnaris* and (possibly) others	Phenoxethol, Methylene Blue, Acriflavine, Chloramphenicol and other antibiotics. Furan, Nifurpyrinol and related compounds are effective but may be potentially dangerous to humans if use is prolonged. Some proprietary remedies available
Whitish growths around the mouth gradually progressing into the jaw bones and anterior cheek area resulting in actual erosion of tissues	Mouth Fungus (name is misleading because the causative agent is not a fungus)	*Flexibacter columnaris* and (possibly) others	As for Fin Rot
Frayed fins, blood spots, ulcers, Exophthalmia (Pop-eye), individually or in combination	Bacteraemia (milder form). Septicaemia (more acute form)	*Aeromonas hydrophila*	Chloramphenicol, Tetracycline, Oxolinic Acid (available in medicated flake form). Some proprietary remedies available
Ulcers (often circular) in head region and/or body	Hole-in-the-head/body. (Ulcer Disease/ Furuncolosis)	*Aeromonas salmonicida* (*A. hydrophila* may act as a secondary agent)	Chloramphenicol, Tetracycline, Sulphonamides, e.g. Furan-based remedy (but see under Fin Rot). Some proprietary remedies available
Any one or combination of: loss of colour/condition, raised scales, Exophthalmia, loss of appetite, emaciation, ulceration, frayed fins	Fish TB	*Mycobacterium* spp	No particularly effective treatment. Some antibiotics, e.g. Terramycin, may effect a cure when infection is not too severe
Swollen abdomen and lifted scales giving the body a 'pine-cone' appearance	Dropsy. (Bacterial haemorrhagic septicaemia)	*Aeromonas liquefaciens* (*ascitae* and/or *typica*); possibly others	Usually no cure but Chloromycetin may help. Humane disposal of affected specimens, plus good hygiene are the most effective methods of eradicating the disease and preventing its recurrence
No external signs of infection but gradual loss of colour, appetite or condition	Non-specific bacterial infection	One or more of the above or other species involved	Phenoxethol, Acriflavine, Methylene Blue, Copper Sulphate, Malachite Green or low dose of a broad-spectrum antibiotic such as Chloramphenicol. Some proprietary remedies available

*1. Commercial non-antibiotic preparations always carry full directions on their use. These must be closely followed to avoid overdosing which can have symptoms and effects as serious as the disease they are designed to treat.
2. Antibiotic remedies are available in certain countries and are supplied with full directions. Where a veterinary surgeon's prescription is necessary, (s)he will supply the relevant details.

PARASITES A parasite is an organism which lives on or in another organism deriving benefit (usually in the form of nutrition) from its host. This type of relationship is strictly one-way since the host never derives any advantage from its association with the invading organism. A strong, healthy individual can carry a certain load of parasites without apparently suffering to any great extent. Should this load become excessive or the host weaker, through environmental or some other form of stress, then the parasites will have a very marked detrimental effect.

According to this broad definition, bacteria and viruses appear to qualify as parasites. When it comes to fish diseases, though, the term 'parasite' is applied just to those organisms, *other than* bacteria or viruses, which have the above relationship with a host. Even so, the range of organisms involved is quite large. It includes fungi (non-green plants related to mushrooms and toadstools), algae, protozoa (single-celled organisms), nematodes (round-worms), crustaceans (related to crabs and lobsters), flukes (trematode worms), cestoids (tapeworms) and acanthocephalids (thorny-headed worms).

Fungi There are relatively few fungal infections of freshwater fish. By far the most common are caused by fungi belonging to the genera *Saprolegnia* and *Achyla*, and are known as Cottonwool Disease or, simply, Fungus. Internal Fungus is caused by *Ichthyophonus hoferi* (formerly known as *Ichthyosporidium*). Less well known is an infection of the gills, known as Gill Rot, caused by species of *Branchiomyces*.

Fungal Infections

Symptoms	Disease	Causative Agents	Some Treatments*
White or cream-coloured fluffy patches on fins and/or body	Cottonwool Disease or Fungus	*Saprolegnia* and *Achyla* species	Proprietary remedies widely available – usually based on Phenoxethol, Malachite Green Copper Sulphate, Potassium Permanganate or Methylene Blue. Salt Bath: 2–5 per cent solution for 10–15 minutes
Variable: Darkened pigmentation sometimes accompanied by curvature of the spine; nodular infection of internal organs; retarded growth; emaciation; loss of balance, giving rise to 'swinging' action; Exophthalmia; scales may have a sand-paper feel; small cysts may appear on the skin	Internal Fungus or Ichthyophonus	*Ichthyophonus hoferi* (formerly *Ichthyosporidium hoferi*)	No definite cure. Antibiotics sometimes have an effect. Phenoxethol has also been used with some success
Yellowish-brown or greyish-white discoloration of gill tissues; impaired breathing; gasping at surface; loss of gill tissue; loss of appetite	Gill Rot or Branchiomycosis	*Branchiomyces sanguinis, B. demigrans*	No effective treatment available. Partial water changes and general improvement of water and stocking conditions should prevent fresh outbreaks. If tank is stripped down, thorough disinfection with proprietary aquarium disinfectant or 1–2 per cent formalin should be carried out

*1. Proprietary non-antibiotic remedies carry full directions which must be followed closely to avoid overdosing.
2. See Bacterial Infections Chart on page 37 concerning use of antibiotics.

Fungal infections almost invariably attack fish that have been pre-weakened by injury, poor environmental conditions, stress (as occurs after spawning), or by a viral, bacterial or parasitic infection. Most species of fungi that cause disease in fish are 'opportunist pathogens' normally living off dead or dying organisms but quickly adapting to living tissues should a suitable opportunity present itself. The infections they cause are, therefore, generally secondary in nature.

Algae Most people are familiar with algae in the form of green or brown encrustations on the rocks and glass in aquaria, as green water or as thin, tough, green filaments which can prove extremely difficult to eradicate. It often comes as a surprise, therefore, to learn that some algae can actually cause diseases in fish. Yet this is not surprising at all when one looks at the incredible diversity that exists among algae. There is, for example, a species, *Gymnodinium microadriaticum*, that lives in the tissues of animals, such as corals, and is absolutely vital to the survival of coral reefs.

Understandably, it is very difficult indeed to define what an alga actually is. It is, perhaps, fair to say that no alga possesses specialised female reproductive structures of the type found in other plants, but even this is a bit of a loose definition.

One particular group of algae, the Dinoflagellates, contains several species which cause diseases among marine and freshwater fish. Dinoflagellates are distinguished from other algae by a combination of factors which include the possession of two whip-like flagella (for swimming) and a stigma (eye-spot). Since many Dinoflagellates are single-celled and motile (free-swimming), some authorities classify them with the protozoa. The Dinoflagellates that affect freshwater fish cause the disease called Velvet. Two species of Velvet are usually recognised: *Oodinium* (*Piscinoodinium*) *limneticum*, which produces a rust-coloured dust-like infestation of the skin, and *O. pillularis*, which is greyish-white in colour. The former remains on the skin of the fish once it (the parasite) has matured and encysts (forms a shell around itself). It then divides into daughter cells which leave the cyst and re-infect the fish. Mature *O. pillularis* drop off the fish and encyst on the bottom of the tank. After replication, the daughter cells leave the cyst and search for a new host. If none is found within 10–12 hours, they will die. Fish that are badly affected by Velvet often die even after treatment. The most effective type of treatment is a salt bath (5 gm per litre) for 1–2 days. Some of the proprietary treatments – Malachite Green, Acriflavine, Methylene Blue or Copper Sulphate – can also help but follow the directions carefully to avoid overdosing.

Protozoa Protozoa are microscopic organisms distinguished from all others in that their bodies consist of a single cell with a well-demarcated nucleus. Although most protozoa possess strictly animal qualities, (such as the ability to swim), some single-celled organisms also carry chlorophyll, the pigment which allows green plants to photosynthesise. This

This Indian Glassfish (*Chanda ranga*) is suffering from a bad attack of Velvet

Protozoan Infections

Symptoms	Disease	Causative Agent	Treatments
Body and fins covered in small white spots; in severe infestations, the spots may appear to join up; fins carried close to the body; violent swimming action or shimmying; scratching against stones, plants and tank equipment	White Spot (Ichthyophthiriasis, or Ich)	*Ichthyophthirius multifiliis*	Numerous proprietary remedies are available, many based on Malachite Green, Methylene Blue or Copper Sulphate. Repeat treatment is often necessary to attack free-swimming stages of the parasite
Slimy, bluish-white coloration of the skin and gills; badly affected areas may show blood spots; awkward swimming movements with fins carried close to the body; scratching, as in White Spot	Costiasis (infectious turbidity of gills and skin)	*Costia necatrix*	These parasites die at 30°C (86°F). Temperature should, therefore, be raised to this level if the affected fish will tolerate it. Acriflavine (10 ml of 0.001 per cent stock solution/5 litres of water); salt (approx. 5 gm/litre): Formalin (approx. 15 ml of 10 per cent stock solution/5 litres for 15–20 minutes). Since free-swimming stages can only survive for about one hour away from a host, affected tanks can be disinfected by removing fish and treating them elsewhere
Symptoms similar to Costiasis; in addition, the skin in the neck to dorsal fin region may develop a lumpy texture; respiration may be impaired	Chilodonelliasis	*Chilodonella cyprini*	Not as sensitive to high temperature as Costia; however, a combination of Acriflavine (1 gm/100 ml of water) at a temperature of 28°C (82°F) for 10 hours is normally effective; Malachite Green (0.15 mg/litre) for an indefinite period. Salt (25 gm/litre for 10–15 minutes or 10–15 gm/litre for 20 minutes); Potassium Permanganate (1 gm/100 litres) for 90 minutes; Methylene Blue (3 ml of 1 per cent solution/10 litres) for an indefinite period
Symptoms similar to Costiasis but usually less severe. Microscopic examination is necessary for definitive diagnosis	Trichodiniasis	*Trichodina domerguei*	As for *Costia* and *Chilodonella*
Sluggish behaviour with occasional sudden swimming movements; emaciation; in extreme	Hexamitiasis/Octomitiasis	*Hexamita/Octomitus* spp.	Dimetridazole (100 mg/litre) for 48 hours; the following drugs have also been effective:

Protozoan Infections (continued)

Symptoms	Disease	Causative Agent	Treatments
cases, small, whitish, worm-like 'plugs' of dead tissue are discharged through the skin leaving small holes; these may develop into larger sores or ulcers			Carbarsone, Calomel, Flagyl and Emtril
Whitish (faded) patches on body; longitudinal coloured body line may break up into patches or virtually disappear; progressive loss of equilibrium	Neon Disease (Plistophorosis/ Plistophoriasis)	*Plistophora (Pleistophora) hyphessobryconis*	No treatment available but improved hygiene often arrests spread of the disease; affected fish usually die quickly
Darkened pigmentation in caudal region; whirling movements; progressive deformity of the backbone; survivors often exhibit (in addition) deformity of the gill covers, mandibles or skull	Whirling Disease	*Myxosoma cerebralis*	This disease is more common in coldwater species; no treatment is available; affected fish should be destroyed and tank disinfected

can make classification rather difficult as mentioned in the preceding section.

Many thousands of protozoan species are known but, fortunately, very few cause diseases in fish. One of these, *Ichthyophthirius multifiliis*, is responsible for what is regarded by many as the most common disease which affects fish – White Spot or Ich. Bearing in mind the universality of bacteria and the internal nature of many of their symptoms, this claim may be a bit difficult to substantiate. What is certainly true is that no aquarist can expect to keep fish on a long-term basis and not experience an outbreak of White Spot at one time or other.

Luckily, there are excellent fast-acting remedies available. This, added to the fact that White Spot is only fatal when the infestation is severe or the fish affected are very weak, makes the disease quite easy to cure. While *Ichthyophthirius* can affect a very large number of species (in fact, no freshwater species can be regarded as being completely immune to attack), other protozoa only cause disease in one, or a few, species of fish. A good example of this is *Plistophora hyphessobryconis* which causes Neon Disease in the Neon (*Paracheirodon innesi*), other Tetras, some Cichlids and several other species.

Having gained a foothold in an aquarium, some protozoan infections can spread quite quickly from fish to fish, irrespective of species, particularly if tank conditions are unfavourable, and can lead to further complications

such as reduced resistance to bacterial attack. Others show a remarkable reluctance to spread between species despite being present in very large numbers. For example, healthy carnivorous/piscivorous species of fish have been experimentally fed on Plistophora-affected fish without developing the disease them-

Cherry Barb with a bad attack of White Spot. Signs of other diseases, e.g. excessive mucus secretion, are also visible

Worm Infections

Symptoms	Disease	Causative Agent	Treatments
Inflamed gills; excessive secretion of mucus on gills; accelerated respiration; gill covers may be held open; scratching of gill covers on plants, rocks and equipment	Gill Fluke Infection	*Dactylogyrus* spp – a Monogenetic Trematode	Some proprietary remedies are available based on a range of compounds, e.g. Copper Sulphate; salt bath (10–15 gm/litre for 20 minutes or 25 gm/litre for 10–15 minutes); Formalin (20 ml commercial formalin/100 litres) for 30–45 minutes; Methylene Blue (3 ml of 1 per cent stock solution/10 litres) indefinitely
Inflamed patches on the skin and fins; erratic swimming; excessive secretion of body slime; accelerated respiration (if gills are affected); some loss of colour; scratching on plants, rocks and equipment	Skin Fluke Infection (may also affect the gills)	*Gyrodactylus* spp – a Monogenetic Trematode	As for *Dactylogrus*
Lumps (cysts) in muscles; mainly among newly imported fish; no apparent discomfort or progression of the symptoms detectable	Internal Fluke Infection (caused by metacercaria – an immature stage in the parasite's life cycle)	Digenetic Trematode, e.g. *Clinostomum*	No effective cure but individual cysts may be removed with a sterile blade or needle and the area disinfected with a proprietary aquarium disinfectant; spontaneous recovery sometimes occurs; fatalities are usually rare
Exhaustion; anaemia (detectable by the pale colour of the gills)	As above	Digenetic Trematode (often *Sanguinicola*)	No effective cure; spread may be prevented by eliminating snails which can act as hosts
Retarded growth; abnormal swelling of abdominal region, sometimes causing lopsidedness; body may lose weight and appear thin despite swollen belly	Tapeworm Infection	A Cestode, e.g. *Ligula*	No treatment available; rare in aquarium species
Pointed red thread-like structures protruding from anus	Roundworm Infection	Nematode – *Camallanus*	No treatment readily available but trichlorphon (1 mg/litre) has sometimes proved effective (check on availability)
Extended abdomen; general debility; one or more worms protruding from abdomen	Roundworm Infection	Nematode – *Capillaria*	As for *Camallanus*
Emaciation; exophthalmia; small bumps may be detectable in the abdominal region	Thorny-headed Worm Infection	An Acanthocephalid	No treatment available, but light infestations can be tolerated by otherwise healthy fish: the infestation may not even be detected

selves, thus confirming the rather limited spreading capabilities of Neon Disease between species (although its spread among members of a susceptible species can be spectacular).

Whatever the invasive/infective abilities of a particular pathogenic organism may be, it is important to identify the causative agent accurately. This is particularly relevant in the case of the internal protozoan infections, such as those caused by *Hexamita* which can have symptoms, e.g. emaciation and loss of appetite, similar to those associated with some bacterial infections. As with many other types of disease, the risk of protozoan infection can be kept low by establishing adequate maintenance routines. *Ichthyophthirius*, for instance, can generally be avoided by ensuring that stress levels are kept under control through proper temperature control (chilling is often associated with outbreaks of this disease) and adequate quarantine procedures in respect of new fish (to prevent the introduction of affected fish into a healthy tank).

Worms Diseases caused by Helminths, such as Flukes, Flatworms, Tapeworms and Nematodes and by Acanthocephala (Thorny-headed Worms) have all been grouped under the single heading of 'Worms' for convenience here although there are significant differences between the various types. While some have simple life cycles, many have highly complicated ones involving one or more intermediate hosts. For example, *Ligula intestinalis*, one of the Tapeworms (Cestodes), has a life cycle which involves two intermediate hosts as well as a final one. The first intermediate host is a freshwater Copepod (a type of crustacean) in which early development of the parasite takes place. When the Copepod is eaten by a fish, development continues inside the abdominal cavity of the second intermediate host. The third stage of the cycle occurs if the fish is, itself, eaten by a bird. When this happens, the parasite can complete its development and attain sexual maturity within a few days in the warm intestine of its final host. Eggs are then discharged in the bird's faeces and they hatch out in the water, thus becoming available once more for consumption by a Copepod.

While there are free-living Helminths, such as some of the Nematodes, e.g. Microworms, *Anguillula silusiae*, used as a livefood for young fish, all the Acanthocephala (Thorny-headed Worms) are parasitic. In those species which are of significance to aquarists, the single intermediate host is, again, a freshwater crustacean. The final host is a fish and the site of attachment is the intestine where considerable damage may be caused.

In addition to these and other internal worm parasites like the Digenetic Trematodes (Internal Flukes), there are also quite a few external ones. The best known of these are the Monogenetic Trematodes (External Flukes) responsible for gill and skin infestations, *Gyrodactylus* and *Dactylogyrus*.

Crustacea Although the vast majority of Crustacea are free-living and many serve as food items for fish, e.g. Brine Shrimp (*Artemia salina*), Freshwater Shrimp (*Gammarus* spp), Fairy Shrimp (*Streptocephalus seali*), Mysid Shrimps and *Cyclops*, a few are important fish parasites which can cause serious problems. The three genera (each with several species) most commonly encountered are *Ergasilus*, *Argulus* and *Lernaea*. The first two are often referred to as the Gill Louse and Fish Louse respectively, while the third is misleadingly known as the Anchor Worm, even though it is not even remotely related to them.

Ergasilus usually affects coldwater fish and will not, therefore, be considered further here. *Argulus*, however, can attack tropical species, although it is often introduced with livefoods collected in ponds in temperate countries during the summer months. This can be quite easily prevented by examining batches of wild-caught livefoods and removing any of the parasites (which can measure nearly 1 cm in length) that may be present. Although light infestations of *Argulus* do not normally cause serious damage, this organism has been linked with the transmission of other diseases such as Fish Pox. *Lernaea* is an unusual parasite in that infestations are caused just by the females.

NON-SPECIFIC DISEASES (INCLUDING MALAWI BLOAT) All

the diseases dealt with in the previous sections can usually be tracked down to one, or a few, definite causative agents. However, there are some diseases which do not fit this category. Listlessness, lethargy, loss of colour, shimmying, Exophthalmia, clamped fins, abnormal pigmentation and other conditions can arise from time to time for no immediately obvious reason and without the apparent intervention of a specific pathogenic organism.

Such 'diseases' are, in fact, symptoms rather than diseases in the strict sense of the word and are usually linked with some unfavourable environmental condition or other. Often, a simple partial water change, alteration in diet, removal of large or aggressive individuals, or the taking of any other step which an analysis

Crustacean Infections

Symptoms	Disease	Causative Agent	Treatments
Nervous swimming and jumpiness; frequent, vigorous scratching against rocks and equipment, often resulting in loss of scales; heavy infestations are accompanied by anaemia and loss of colour; the almost-transparent parasites can be seen attached to the body mainly along the fin bases (adult parasites can be nearly 1 cm long)	Fish Louse Infection	*Argulus* spp – usually *A. foliaceus*	Organophosphate bath (e.g. Dipterex or Naled – follow instructions closely); Potassium Permanganate (1 gm/litre for 30–45 seconds or 1 gm/10 litres for 5–10 minutes); physical removal of individual parasites with forceps followed by disinfection with a proprietary disinfectant, e.g. an Acriflavine-based compound
Long, thin, white, worm-like parasites (up to 2 cm in length) attached to the body and/or fins; two white egg-sacs at the posterior end are usually visible	Anchor Worm Infection	*Lernaea* spp	Some proprietary remedies are available, e.g. based on Copper Sulphate; Potassium Permanganate – as for *Argulus*. Salt bath (10–15 gm/litre for 20 minutes or 25 gm/litre for 10–15 minutes); Trichlorphon (1 mg/litre) indefinitely may also dislodge the parasite (check on availability)

of the maintenance regime may indicate, is sufficient to remedy the situation. Therefore, unless the cause of a presumed disease is known, a systematic examination of conditions within an aquarium should be considered as the first mandatory step in tackling non-specific cases.

One particular non-specific disease that has been causing considerable problems among African Cichlid hobbyists is Malawi Bloat. This condition was first recorded in African Rift Lake Cichlids in the mid-1970s in stocks originating from Lake Malawi. As the range of Rift Lake species expanded, so did the occurrence of Bloat, so that it is now known to occur in fish from other African Lakes besides Lake Malawi.

The disease is unusual in several ways not least in that mouthbrooding species seem to be the only ones affected. As the name suggests, affected fish develop a bloated abdomen, often accompanied by raised scales (as in dropsy). Death can occur within 12 hours of the first symptoms appearing or can take up to a week. There is no known definitive cure for Malawi Bloat simply because (at the time of writing) its causative agent, or agents, cannot be pinpointed. Bacteria, viruses, soft or acid water (Rift Lake Cichlids require hardish, alkaline condi-

tions), diet, stress and other factors have all been implicated. Although affected fish die, it has sometimes been possible to arrest the spread of the disease by altering the diet, establishing appropriate water conditions, reducing the level of stress and generally improving the maintenance routine.

In the end, Malawi Bloat may prove to be a combination of diseases caused by a combination of factors which exist in aquaria but not in the wild. Even though, so far, it has not been recorded in wild populations, it is theoretically possible that affected fish may fall foul of predators quickly under natural conditions, thus being unlikely to be found by collectors or divers.

Disease Prevention

The old addage, 'Prevention is better than cure', is just as relevant to fish as to humans. As has already been emphasised, one's efforts should primarily be directed towards maintaining healthy fish. Even when this is the case, outbreaks of disease will occur from time to time. However, these occurrences will be infrequent and, if the symptoms are diagnosed early, most potentially serious consequences can be avoided.

It is true to say that aquaria generally house a range of potentially dangerous pathogenic agents. Frightening though this may sound to some, the situation is, in reality, no different to our own lives. As long as we take reasonable care, we do not normally go from one crisis to another, running through the whole army of pathogens which surround and invade us. It is the same with fish. It is important to stress this to reassure anyone who has begun to wonder how fish can possibly survive at all after reading the details of diseases dealt with in earlier sections!

Fish cannot move out of the accommodation that we provide for them. Therefore, we should bear this in mind and behave accordingly. As long as we do this, our hobby will live up to its potential. If we ignore the basic rules, then serious outbreaks of disease, accompanied by their distressing consequences, will inevitably follow. The sad thing about this is that such situations can generally be avoided with a little thought and consideration.

Summary Chart of Main Preventative Measures

1. Check on food, temperature and water requirements of individual species *before* purchase.
2. Check on compatibility of species before purchase, e.g. large Angels (*Pterophyllum scalare*) and small Neons (*Paracheirodon innesi*) should not be kept together.
3. Take into consideration behavioural characteristics when choosing fish. For example: Do males fight? Can males and females be kept together all the time? Is the species in question timid/aggressive?
4. When buying shoaling species, e.g. Cardinals (*Paracheirodon axelrodi*), get at least six individuals.
5. Do not overstock the tank with fish.
6. Do not understock the tank with plants.
7. Do not overfeed.
8. Provide adequate shelter in the form of dense clumps of vegetation and/or caves for timid individuals and species.
9. Allow tap to run for several minutes before drawing water for an aquarium.
10. Treat raw water with dechlorinators and other conditioners.
11. Carry out regular partial water changes, e.g. 20 per cent every 10–14 days.
12. Always equilibrate old and new water temperatures when carrying out water changes or introducing new fish.
13. Check pH and nitrite levels about once a fortnight (daily during the first few weeks) and alter accordingly.
14. Carry out changes in temperature, pH, hardness, nitrite levels or any other parameters *gradually*.
15. Avoid other potentially stressful situations, e.g. excessive chasing/netting of fish, abrupt switching on/off of tank lights (particularly at night).
16. Avoid contamination of water with toxic fumes, e.g. paint, furniture polish, aerosols, etc.
17. Keep a separate net for each tank and disinfect it regularly with a proprietary aquarium disinfectant.
18. Select healthy fish, i.e. those which appear alert, carry their fins erect, are colourful, full-bodied and undamaged.
19. Quarantine *all* new fish.

QUARANTINE As stated earlier, fish are surrounded by potentially harmful pathogens. This applies both to home and shop aquaria. The mere physical act of netting in the shop, followed by bagging, transport and debagging into an alien environment at home can cause sufficient stress in a fish to reduce its resistance to the point where it becomes highly susceptible to attack. Therefore, when such a fish is released into an established tank and is required, on top of everything else, to compete with the resident fish for food and space, it is bound to experience some problems. It does not, of course, follow that every new fish will develop some disease or other. In fact, many fish are so resilient that they will survive this traumatic period in their lives quite successfully.

However, the inherent risks cannot be overlooked and it makes sense to take precautions, particularly since apparently healthy fish can be harbouring dangerous parasites or bacteria. A period of quarantine lasting approximately two weeks is usually long enough to allow fish to settle down, recover from their shop-to-home ordeal, get used to their new water and, very importantly, exhibit signs of any disease which they may be carrying.

When a new tank is set up, it can automatically provide quarantine accommodation for the first batch of fish. This is not an ideal situation but it, nevertheless, often works quite effectively. Problems arise, though, if any of the fish in this first batch are carrying a serious disease such as TB. In such cases, or in others where complete disinfection is required and plants need to be destroyed, the experience invariably proves both depressing and time-consuming. Fortunately, selecting healthy, acclimatised or quarantined fish which are known to be feeding well in the shop will reduce risks very considerably.

Few aquarists, if any, obtain all the fish they are ever likely to require in a single batch. New fish are regularly being bought to replace those that die (for whatever reason) or to increase the collection. Since each new purchase is a potential source of trouble, steps have to be taken to minimise the risks. It is on such occasions that the value of a quarantine tank becomes obvious. Although some new aquarists may bemoan the extra expense, it only takes one major wipe-out to convince them that it is most unwise to dispense with a quarantine tank. Luck and good general aquarium management may result in prolonged success even without a quarantine tank and this may well lull the aquarist into a false sense of security. Sooner or later, though, disaster will strike. If, by that time, the aquarist has progressed to rare, difficult or expensive species, (s)he will have yet more reasons to regret not having followed this golden rule of fish-keeping.

While there is no denying that a quarantine tank represents a supplementary expense, this needs to be put into perspective.

1. Every aquarist should have a spare tank, heater, thermostat, inexpensive filter and airstone ready for use in case of emergencies. Therefore, setting up a quarantine tank (which does not have to be either as large or sophisticated as the main tank) should be seen as one of the normal precautionary steps that every aquarist should take as a matter of course, rather than as a luxury item.
2. When not used for quarantine purposes, the tank can still be used to isolate and treat sick fish in; to isolate pregnant livebearer females; as a breeding tank for individual pairs of egglayers; and for the raising of fry.

As mentioned earlier, *all* new fish should be quarantined. This applies even to those that have been bought from a dealer who quarantines his/her fish, since the stresses generated during the transaction will affect these fish as much as any other. The great advantage of buying quarantined fish is that they are, obviously, less likely to give rise to problems. These would have been evident in the dealer's tanks and should have been tackled well before the fish are offered for sale. In such cases, the quarantine period at home can be reduced to

around one week in reasonable safety. Other fish require at least one week more. If no problems arise at the end of the fortnight, then introduction into the main tank can be carried out (preferably in the evening, shortly before lights out, to allow the fish several hours of relative peace before they start competing with the resident population). If, however, any signs of disease become apparent, even if only a single specimen is affected, the whole batch undergoing quarantine must be treated. Once the symptoms have disappeared, one to two further weeks should be allowed as a safety measure.

Just because a tank is being primarily used for quarantine purposes, this does not mean that it has to *look* like a hospital! My own quarantine tanks are just as attractive as my show tanks, the only difference being that they do not have any absorbent materials in them such as bogwood. Instead, the shelters are built of simulated rock/wood made out of glass fibre which can be scrubbed and disinfected easily. Undergravel filtration is pointless in a quarantine tank since the beneficial bacteria that these filters depend on can be killed by some of the remedies which may need to be employed, giving rise to even more problems. Adequate aeration, accompanied by partial water changes, are, therefore, quite sufficient in most cases.

Conclusions

The diseases dealt with in this chapter represent only a fraction of the total number known to afflict fish. The lists of symptoms and treatments presented cannot, therefore, be considered to be exhaustive.

The study of fish diseases and, equally important, fish health, is a huge and expanding subject, often requiring highly specialised knowledge to distinguish between superficially similar, but fundamentally different, symptoms. Despite this, it is hoped that the details presented in the previous pages will prove of assistance in diagnosing and treating the majority of diseases that are likely to arise in home aquaria. The emphasis, though, must be in preventing dangerous situations developing. Should this fail, and should the observed symptoms be difficult to diagnose, expert advice should be sought from a veterinary surgeon without delay. In countries where the use of certain drugs, such as antibiotics, is either restricted or prohibited by law, consultation with a vet should be considered essential even when the symptoms of diseases requiring such medications are correctly diagnosed.

Fish Reproduction

However successful one is at setting up and maintaining attractive, well-balanced aquaria, and however rewarding the exercise and experience might be, this cannot be regarded as the pinnacle of aquatic achievement. Most experienced aquarists agree that the successful breeding of aquarium fish marks an even higher level of attainment and, consequently, provides an even deeper and more fulfilling sense of enjoyment.

Breeding success is generally accepted as a sign that the fish are being kept in a favourable environment and are content. While it may be difficult to prove whether fish are content or not, it seems reasonable to assume that breeding success will be either non-existent, or nearly so, if conditions are unfavourable. 'Unfavourable' must not be taken to be synonymous with dirty or unattractive aquaria, though. In fact, a sparkling, devastatingly beautiful set-up can be extremely unfavourable if it overlooks the needs of the species in question. For example, an otherwise perfect aquarium would be most unsuitable for breeding Discus if the pH of the water were to be anywhere above neutral, i.e. above 7. Equally, a spectacular aquarium with acid water, i.e. pH below 7, will be found unacceptable by most, if not all, the African Rift Lake Cichlids. The message is, therefore, clear: the setting up of an aquarium for breeding purposes must be based on a sound knowledge of the reproductive and other characteristics of the fish.

Reproductive Strategies

One of the traditional methods of classifying aquarium fish is by means of their method of reproduction, i.e. their reproductive strategy. This results in a two-fold division:

1. **Livebearers:** these species do not lay eggs; fertilisation is internal and the females retain the developing embryos within their body cavity up to the moment of birth.
2. **Egglayers:** these species release their eggs into the water where they are fertilised; embryonic development, therefore, takes place outside the female's body.

As with every other rule, there are exceptions. For example, some sharks, skates and rays employ internal fertilisation but then release their eggs into the water where they complete their development. Other sharks, however, retain their eggs internally up to the moment of birth. There is even a Characin, *Corynopoma riisei* (the Swordtail Characin), a Poeciliid (the family to which Guppies belong), *Tomeurus gracilis*, and a few Killifish, e.g. *Cynolebias brucei*, that have developed this reproductive strategy, known technically as ovi-ovoviviparity. However, for the vast majority of aquarium species, the above division can be regarded as valid.

Livebearers

There are five main types of aquarium livebearers.

1. The Poeciliids (Family: Poeciliidae) represented by the majority of aquarium species, such as Guppies (*Poecilia reticulata*), Mollies (*P. sphenops, latipinna* and *velifera*), Swordtails (*Xiphophorus helleri*) and Platies (*X. maculatus* and *variatus*).
2. The Anablepids (Family: Anablepidae) represented by the various species of Four-eyed Fish (*Anableps* spp).
3. The Jenynsiids (Family: Jenynsiidae) represented by a single species, the One-sided Livebearer (*Jenynsia lineata*).
4. The Goodeids (Family: Goodeidae) represented by about 37 species, the most popular being the Butterfly Goodeid (*Ameca splendens*) and the Orange-tailed Goodeid (Xenotoca eiseni).
5. The *Hemiramphids* (Family: Exocoetidae) represented by several species known collectively as Halfbeaks. The most popular are species of the genera *Dermogenys* and *Nomorhamphus*.

On the whole, it is quite easy to spawn livebearers (*Anableps* is an exception). In fact, the difficulty with some of them lies in preventing them from breeding. Despite individual differences in the number and size of young produced, one rule about the livebearer breeding tank is that it should contain adequate shelter in the form of dense clumps of fine-leaved vegetation, such as *Cabomba*, *Myriophyllum* (Milfoil) or *Vesicularia dubyana* (Java Moss). A thick layer of floating plants like *Salvinia* or *Riccia* should also be provided. Alternatively, females may be placed in a breeding trap when they are close to giving birth. The reason for these precautions is that livebearers are generally cannibalistic towards their own young. Even predominantly vegetarian species, such as Mollies, will often make a meal out of their offspring.

A pair of Poeciliids, *Xiphophorus xiphidium* (male on left)

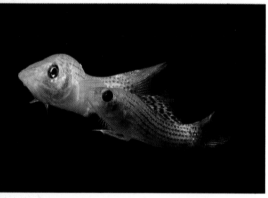

A pair of Sailfin Mollies in the act of mating

Livebearers, e.g. *Girardinichthys viviparus*, produce huge fry

How to Recognise a Livebearer Since livebearers fertilise their eggs internally, they must, obviously, have the necessary anatomical adaptations to allow them to carry out this process satisfactorily. The most easily distinguishable of these is a series of elongated rays that male Poeciliids, Anablepids and Jenynsiids have in their anal fins. In addition, male Poeciliids carry structures known as spines, hooks, claws and blades on these rays. In all three types of fish, the copulatory organ formed by the modified anal fin is called a gonopodium. In Goodeid males, the modifications are considerably simpler and merely consist of a shortening and condensing of the first few rays of the fin. This results in a notched copulatory organ known as a spermatopodium. In the Halfbeaks, the modified anal fin of the males is known as an andropodium.

Female livebearers have normally shaped anal fins, making the use of this characteristic for identification purposes next to useless. However, as gestation progresses, pregnant females (which are referred to as 'gravid') of many species develop darker pigmentation of the abdominal area closest to the genital aperture. This gravid spot has a characteristic colour, size and shape which is virtually unique to each species and can, therefore, be used to distinguish between otherwise very similar-looking females.

How to Recognise a Female Livebearer About to Give Birth After the eggs have been fertilised, livebearer females will retain them for a period which can be as short as less than four weeks or as long as eight weeks or more. The duration of the gestation period will depend on a number of factors ranging from the species concerned to the temperature of the water. As mentioned earlier, most livebearers are cannibalistic towards their own offspring. It is, therefore, important to recognise the signs that are associated with the stages immediately preceding birth so that adequate steps can be taken. If the actual date on which the female was mated is known, then she can be placed in a breeding trap or in a separate, densely planted tank approximately one week before she is due to drop her fry. If this proves impractical, it is still quite possible to take steps to save the fry if signs of imminent birth can be recognised.

As the female goes through the very last stages of gestation, she will become particularly attractive to males, probably through secretions produced as the embryos hatch out from their follicles (egg sacs) or as the genital aperture prepares itself for the birth. As a

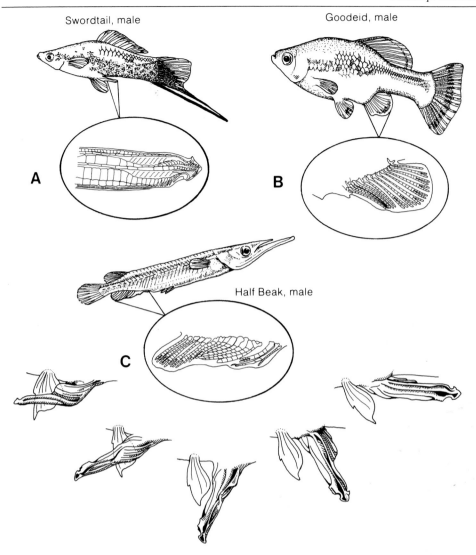

Swordtail, male

Goodeid, male

A

B

Half Beak, male

C

The anal fins of livebearing males are modified into copulatory (mating) organs. *Top left:* Poeciliid male. (A) Gonopodium. *Top right*: Goodeid male. (B) Spermatopodium. *Centre*: Half Beak male. (C) Andropodium. *Bottom sequence*: (right to left) The swing of a Poeciliid gonopodium from the resting to the mating position (modified from Rosen & Gordon, 1953)

result, females at the point of giving birth are often more persistently chased by males of their own species than at any other time during the gestation period. The genital aperture itself usually becomes more prominent or pointed during this time and the anal fin often exhibits a change in coloration, e.g. it can become darker or streaky.

In Goodeids, the fully developed embryos become very active just before birth and begin to wriggle, sometimes quite vigorously, inside the ovarian cavity. These movements can be seen very clearly from the outside and can be taken as a definite sign that birth is either imminent or already under way.

Types of Livebearing

There are two basic types of livebearing:

1. *Ovoviviparity:* the eggs are fertilised while still in their egg sacs (follicles) where they remain until they hatch just before birth. The embryos do not increase significantly in weight during gestation.

2. *Viviparity:* the eggs are fertilised in the follicles but are ejected into the ovarian cavity soon afterwards where they complete their development. The embryos undergo a significant weight increase during gestation.

As with all definitions, there are difficulties with the above categorisations. There is, for a start, the difficulty of defining the word 'significant'. Further, in the Poeciliid, *Heterandria formosa*, a species of Mosquito Fish, and in *Anableps*, the Four-eyed Fish, the embryos experience significant weight increases (by any standards) in spite of the fact that gestation is of the follicular type. In addition, *Heterandria formosa* and several other related livebearers, such as some of the *Poeciliopsis* species, do not produce single, large batches of fry every few weeks like other livebearers do. Instead, they drop fry on a regular basis, in batches which can consist of as few as one or two specimens. This reproductive strategy is known as superfoetation. Despite the imperfections outlined above, one can safely say that the majority of livebearers are of the ovoviviparous type.

Ovoviviparous aquarium fish exhibit a further series of interesting characteristics. For instance, males will produce their sperm in packets called spermatozeugmata (in truly viviparous species, like the Goodeids, sperm are produced free). Some of the spermatozeugmata will be used by the recipient female to fertilise her first batch of ripe eggs. However, she will also store the remaining sperm until she releases the first batch of fry several weeks later, and will then utilise them to fertilise a fresh batch of eggs. This remarkable ability allows ovoviviparous females to produce a series of broods (sometimes as many as ten) at regular intervals without the need for repeated mating. In Goodeids, this is not possible, each brood arising from a separate insemination.

Irrespective of whether a livebearer is ovoviviparous or viviparous, the fact that the eggs and embryos are carried inside the female during gestation provides each offspring with a considerable degree of protection. The only real danger, of course, arises when the female finds herself at risk from predators or disease. Under normal circumstances,. however, the degree of protection is such that livebearers can afford (in survival terms) to reduce the number of fry produced in each brood. This means that the total amount of available yolk, or other form of nutrition, can be divided between fewer individuals than is usually the case with egglayers. Consequently, the developing embryos of most livebearing species can grow to a larger relative size and develop more fully before birth than their egglayer counterparts. Both these characteristics are clearly visible at birth and make the rearing of such fry a relatively easy matter compared to the task of raising most egglayer fry from birth to adult. The common livebearers, therefore, provide aquarists with a golden opportunity of experiencing success even during the earliest stages of fishkeeping.

Egglayers

The scientific term for the most common type of egglaying exhibited by fish is Oviparity. Its main characteristics are:

1. Eggs and sperm are shed into the water by the spawning pair or shoal;
2. Fertilisation is, therefore, external;
3. Entire embryonic development occurs outside the parents' bodies. (Since the internal body environment begins in the throat region, even mouthbrooders, technically, incubate their eggs externally.)
4. Developing embryos derive all their nourishment from the yolk present in the egg.

Stages 1 and 2, above, distinguish true oviparity from ovi-ovoviviparity (delayed egglaying).

Although all egglaying species exhibit the same characteristics in terms of egg fertilisation and embryonic nutrition, the methods by which this is achieved are even more wide-ranging than those found among livebearers. It is, therefore, absolutely essential to obtain as much information as possible about individual species before making any spawning attempts.

How to Recognise an Egglayer Egglayers, obviously, do not require the specialised fin adaptations that livebearers do, since the job of egg fertilisation outside the body is usually more simple. There has, therefore, generally been little or no evolutionary pressure on these species towards the development of extravagant, complicated, anatomical fin modifications. This does not, however, mean that male and female egglayers always have virtually identical finnage. This does occur, as in many Tetras (Family: Characidae), but, equally often, there are marked differences in either fin colour, size, or both, between the sexes.

When there *are* marked differences in finnage, such as in those Mouthbrooding Cichlids (Family: Cichlidae) where the males have elongated anal fin rays which culminate in egg-like mimics (egg dummies), the structure of the fin can invariably be seen to be inappropriate for internal fertilisation. It is, therefore, quite possible even for newcomers to the hobby of fishkeeping to identify a species as an egglayer simply by noting the absence of any of the anal fin modifications outlined earlier in the section on livebearers. (See page 47 for details of some of the few exceptions to the rule.)

Male Peacock Cichlid (*Aulonocara* sp) showing characteristic mouthbrooding egg spots on the anal fin

Pair of *Astatotilapia burtoni* spawning. The female is taking a batch of eggs into her mouth.
(See pages 53–54 for fuller details.)

The female is seen pecking at the egg spots on the male's anal fin, thus stimulating him to release sperm

Female *A. burtoni* with fry. These will be taken into the female's mouth if danger threatens

How to Recognise Egglayers in Breeding Condition In most cases, there is no significant difference in coloration between livebearers in or out of breeding condition. In egglayers, the situation is much more variable. Some species, for example, exhibit no difference in coloration to speak of. This is usually the case with egg-scattering species like the Neon Tetra (*Paracheirodon innesi*) and Cardinal Tetra (*P. axelrodi*). Nevertheless, females in breeding condition can be easily picked out by their fullness of body which clearly indicates that they are ripe with eggs.

In the majority of species where some form of parental care of eggs and/or young occurs, there is often a pronounced difference between male and female finnage which may or may not be accompanied by corresponding differences in body coloration. (Discus, *Symphysodon* spp, and Angels, *Pterophyllum scalare,* are two exceptions.)

There can also be equally large colour differences between fish in and out of breeding

condition. Non-breeding colours, however attractive they might be, are never as intense or spectacular as those developed in the period leading up to spawning or during actual spawning itself.

In many species, such as some Loricariid Catfishes (Family: Loricariidae), males develop nuptial growths rather than nuptial coloration, in this case taking the form of whiskers. In other kinds of fish, the growths appear as tiny pimples called nuptial tubercles. The best-known example of this is the ubiquitous Goldfish, *Carassius auratus*. In the various species of Salmon, *Salmo* spp, males develop fatty humps in the neck region and hooked vicious-looking jaws, called kypes. In fact, there are so many forms of nuptial adaptations that no aquarist will ever be able to observe more than a fraction of them in a lifetime of fishkeeping.

Irrespective of whether there is a visible physical change or not, egglayers in breeding condition can be recognised by their behaviour. There are so many variations on the reproductive theme, that the best way in which this behaviour can be described to cover all eventualities is that it shows a pronounced departure from normal day-to-day behaviour. This can take the form of intensified chasing of females by males in egg-scattering species, increased aggression towards all comers by a potential breeding pair, accompanied by the establishment of a territory, preparation of a nest site, construction of a nest, or any one of countless interesting permutations.

Types of Egglaying

Numerous attempts have been made over the years to classify the bewildering array of reproductive strategies exhibited by egglayers. These reproductive classifications, of course, do not necessarily correspond with the wider, systematic classification which places individual species within genera, genera within families, and so on. Consequently, we find that species which belong to the same family may well appear under separate slots in reproductive terms. For example, the family Belon-

The Cichlid *Neetropus nematopus* shows marked differences between normal (above) and reproductive coloration

tiidae includes species such as the Siamese Fighting Fish (*Betta splendens*), the Dwarf Gourami (*Colisa lalia*) and the Chocolate Gourami (*Sphaerichthys osphromenoides*). However, in any classification based on reproductive strategies, the first two would feature under the nest-building category, while the last would appear alongside other mouthbrooders.

Ignoring all other parameters, there are four major types of egglayers:

1. Species with pelagic eggs, i.e. eggs that are free-floating or drifting – no freshwater tropical aquarium species fall within this category.
2. Species with demersal eggs but no parental care of either eggs or offspring, i.e. eggs laid on the bottom or another suitable medium but then abandoned. Examples: Tetras, Carps (including Rasboras and Barbs), Killifish and many other aquarium species.
3. Species with demersal eggs and some degree of parental protection. Examples: Many Cichlids (not mouthbrooders), most Gouramis, some Catfishes and others.
4. Species that carry their eggs or young (externally, as opposed to internally as in livebearers). Examples: Mouthbrooding Cichlids, some Catfishes, some Anabantoids, Rice Fishes and others.

The fact that all these strategies exist is (literally) living proof that they are all successful. They are, in fact, different but equally 'correct' solutions to the overriding problem of species survival. Each solution, therefore, has its own characteristics.

Species with Demersal Eggs but no Parental Care Eggs have to be produced in sufficiently large quantities to ensure that, at least, two individuals will survive to adulthood, thus replacing their parents and maintaining the size of the population constant. The eggs of these species are often very difficult to see, as in most Barbs, or are hidden from view, as in many Killifish.

Species with Demersal Eggs and Some Degree of Parental Protection This category contains the widest range of egglaying reproductive strategies. Some species merely clean a suitable spawning site and lay their eggs upon it, e.g. many South American Cichlids, like the Angel (*Pterophyllum scalare*) which deposits its eggs on a leaf, or the Oscar (*Astronotus ocellatus*) which uses a flattish rock. In the Splashing Tetra (*Copella* spp), the eggs are actually laid on a leaf several centimetres *above* the water surface.

Other species build a nest instead of cleaning a suitable spawning site. This can take many forms, ranging from the simple depressions excavated by many Cichlids to the elaborate bubblenests at the water surface or under submerged objects constructed by most Gouramis and some Catfishes.

Species That Carry Their Eggs or Young The duration or intensity of this type of egg protection varies greatly. In the various species of Rice Fish or Medakas (*Oryzias* spp), fertilised eggs are carried by the females suspended from their genital aperture until a suitable medium is found, usually fine-leaved vegetation, whereupon the eggs are rubbed off and left to complete their development.

In Mouthbrooding Cichlids, however, the female takes the eggs into her mouth almost as soon as they are laid. She also attempts to take in the egg spots or dummies which the male has on his anal fin. In so doing, she sucks in sperm released by the male and, thus, ensures the fertilisation of the eggs. The developing eggs will be kept by the female inside her mouth until they hatch. She will then release the fry

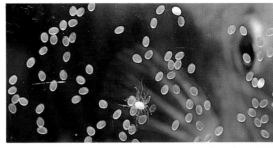

A batch of Discus eggs laid on the front of an aquarium. A few are unfertilised and have developed Fungus

This pair of *Cichlasoma panamense* are protecting their brood of fry (visible along the bottom of the photograph)

A male *Sturisoma panamensis* guarding three batches of developing eggs. Some from the lowest group have hatched

A shoal of healthy young Discus still being looked after by one of the parent fish

A 10-day-old *Sturisoma panamensis* Catfish. Compare its small size with parent partly visible in the background

once they become free-swimming but will continue to offer them protection, for a time, inside her mouth should danger threaten.

As in livebearers, the intense protection which these species offer their young is such that they can afford to produce fewer offspring per brood than, say, egg scatterers. Lower numbers also make it possible for each egg to receive a larger amount of yolk, thus allowing each embryo to develop to a larger size and to a more advanced stage than would otherwise be the case. For relative newcomers to fishkeeping, therefore, Mouthbrooding Cichlids will provide a better chance of early spawning success than many of the other types of egglayers whose tiny, under-developed fry can often present a serious challenge even to established aquarists.

Livebearers and Egglayers Compared

Type	Fertilisation	Incubation	Embryonic Nutrition	External Diagnostic Features
Livebearers	Internal	Internal	From egg yolk and/or maternal secretions	Males have modified anal fin, e.g. gonopodium, used for mating
Egglayers	External	External	Exclusively from egg yolk	Anal fin of males not modified for internal fertilisation

Reproductive Strategies and Representative Species

Strategy	Common Name	Scientific Name
Livebearers		
(i) Ovoviviparous	Guppy	*Poecilia reticulata*
	Swordtail	*Xiphophorus helleri*
	Platy	*Xiphophorus maculatus* and *X. variatus*
	Molly	*Poecilia sphenops, P. latipinna* and *P. velifera*
(ii) Viviparous	One-sided Livebearer	*Jenynsia lineata*
	Butterfly Goodeid	*Ameca splendens*
	Orange-tailed Goodeid	*Xenotoca eiseni*
(iii) Species exhibiting characteristics of (i) and (ii)	Mosquito Fish	*Heterandria formosa*
	Four-eyed Fish	*Anableps* spp
Egglayers		
(i) Species with pelagic eggs	No aquarium representatives	
(ii) Species with demersal eggs but no parental care	Neon Tetra	*Paracheirodon innesi*
	Cardinal Tetra	*Paracheirodon axelrodi*
	Mexican Tetra/ Blind Cave Fish	*Astyanax fasciatus mexicanus*
	Zebra Danio	*Brachydanio rerio*
	Tiger Barb	*Barbus tetrazona*
	Argentine Pearl Fish	*Cynolebias bellotti*
(iii) Species with demersal eggs and parental care	Angel Fish	*Pterophyllum scalare*
	Jewel Cichlid	*Hemichromis bimaculatus*
	Kribensis	*Pelvicachromis pulcher*
	Oscar	*Astronotus ocellatus*
	Discus	*Symphysodon* spp
	Dwarf Gourami	*Colisa lalia*
	Blue Gourami	*Trichogaster trichopterus*
	Siamese Fighting Fish	*Betta splendens*
(iv) Species that carry their eggs or young	Rice Fish/Medaka	*Oryzias latipes*
	South African Mouthbrooder	*Pseudocrenilâbrus philander*
	Golden Nyasa Cichlid	*Melanochromis auratus*
	Chocolate Gourami	*Sphaerichthys osphromenoides*
	Bronze Catfish	*Corydoras aeneus*

The Aquarium

When an aquarium is described as 'tropical', it is usually assumed to be 'one in which fish and plants from tropical parts of the world are housed'. Yet, when we look at this broad classification in a little more detail, some flaws begin to become apparent. How, for instance, do we define 'tropical'? Where do we actually draw the line?

All countries that are located between the Tropics of Cancer and Capricorn, and the fish that are found in them, can be said to be tropical without too much fear of contradiction. For example, Brazil and its fishes are universally regarded as being tropical. China, on the other hand, is regarded differently. Yet the Paradise Fish (*Macropodus opercularis*) found there and in Taiwan, Korea and South Vietnam is usually thought of as a tropical fish, although it can withstand cool temperatures.

There are, in addition, other species which can withstand temperatures below those normally considered in the aquarium hobby to represent the tropical range, i.e. about 22°c (71.5°F) and above. For example, Rosy Barbs (*Barbus conchonius*) can tolerate a temperature of around 15°c (59°F) quite comfortably during the winter months. However, they cannot breed at this temperature and it is this criterion that may be considered the critical one.

In general terms, therefore, a tropical aquarium requires the provision of artificial heat for the successful breeding of most of the species it contains. This is, of course, a relative definition. This is because its heating aspect applies fully to temperate countries but not to tropical ones as defined above (although even in these countries heating is required at high altitudes).

Basic Tropical Aquarium Requirements

In order to provide adequate conditions for most tropical fish and plants, an aquarium must be adequately heated, illuminated and aerated, and must contain water of appropriate chemical composition and quality.

Heating The only absolute rule concerning heating aquaria is that the source of heat must be *dependable and safe*. Therefore, as long as these conditions are met, the aquarist is free to choose whatever means are available or thought to be suitable. If numerous aquaria need to be heated, then space heating, i.e. heating the room rather than the individual aquaria, may be the best choice.

Since hot air rises, tanks placed on high shelves will be warmer than those lower down. Therefore, a range of temperatures can be created to suit individual species or conditions, e.g. breeding, without the need to install separate heaters and thermostats in every aquarium. While such an arrangement is quite suitable for the multiple-tank owner, most aquarists, particularly new ones, usually have a single aquarium or just a few. In fact, even if the idea is to become a large-scale aquarist, absolute beginners would be well advised to begin with a single tank and concentrate on mastering the basic but essential skills of aquarium management before diversifying along more ambitious lines.

The single-tank aquarist can dispense with space heating arrangements, heat exchangers and the like, although it will prove advantageous if the aquarium is located in a normally heated room in the house. Such rooms are generally subject to relatively small temperature fluctuations which, in turn, result in an increased level of stability within the aquarium itself. This makes temperature control easier and can, in some cases, prolong the life of the aquarium heater and thermostat significantly.

Choosing an appropriate heating unit is, obviously, very important. As one would expect, heaters and thermostats are available in a range of designs, each with its own advantages and disadvantages. Some are very sophisticated and include easy-to-adjust, accurate controls; others may be somewhat more basic and not so accurate, but still quite suitable for most purposes. These differences are, of course, reflected in the price and the aquarist must make the final decision, as long as the chosen equipment can do the required job comfortably and have sufficient reserve capacity to handle unforeseen problems, such as the total breakdown of the central heating system in the house.

The most popular type of heating equipment is the combined heater and thermostat unit usually referred to as the heater-stat. Other types include internal, small heating plates with external (to the aquarium) thermostatic control, external base plates of various sizes to fit standard aquaria, and internal sub-gravel heating cables. The great advantage externally adjustable units have over internal ones is that temperature alterations can be carried out without having to remove the unit from the

water, simply by turning a knob in the required direction. Internal units, for their part, are usually cheaper and just as dependable, even though temperature adjustments may prove a bit more awkward to control in some of the models.

Once the decision concerning the type of heating unit has been made, the next obvious step is to choose a heater of sufficient wattage to perform the required job satisfactorily. Manufacturers usually, but not invariably, provide guidelines for a range of aquarium sizes. If these are not included, approximate wattages can be estimated by working out the capacity of the aquarium in gallons (Imperial or US) and multiplying this by 10 for aquaria up to 60 cm

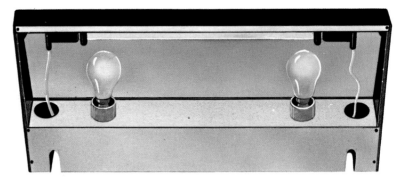

Aquarium hoods are normally designed to house lighting units: this one holds a fluorescent tube and two tungsten bulbs

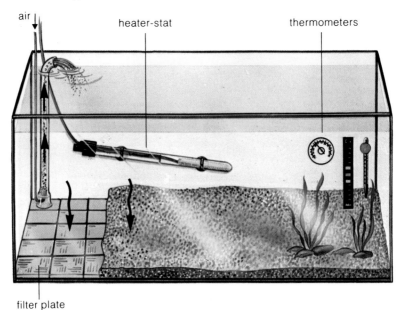

Diagram showing the principle of underground filtration. Also shown are a heater-stat and three types of thermometer

air

heater-stat

thermometers

filter plate

(24 in) in length, by 6 for aquaria up to 120 cm (48 in) and by 4 for those larger than this.

It must be stressed that figures obtained in this way are only approximate. However, they work out on the generous side and will prove perfectly adequate for most situations. If the room in which an aquarium is housed is either cool or subject to moderate temperature fluctuations, the wattages suggested in the accompanying table should be increased by 50 per cent. In extreme cases where no room heat is available and temperatures either drop dramatically or are permanently low during the colder months of the year, double the suggested wattage should be adequate to maintain tropical conditions in aquaria. It could, of course, be argued that tropical aquaria should be set up to be admired and should not, therefore, be placed in a cold, inhospitable room.

Approximate Heating Requirements for Aquaria Kept in Heated/Warm Rooms

Aquarium Size

Inches	Approx. metric equivalent (cm)	Total wattage
18×10×10	45×25×25	30– 60
24×12×12	60×30×30	75–100
36×12×15	90×30×37	100–150
48×15×15	120×30×37	120–180
60×18×18	150×45×45	150–210

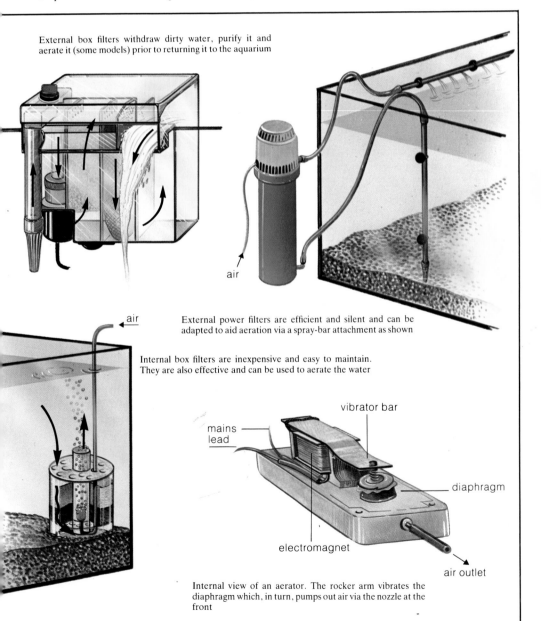

External box filters withdraw dirty water, purify it and aerate it (some models) prior to returning it to the aquarium

External power filters are efficient and silent and can be adapted to aid aeration via a spray-bar attachment as shown

Internal box filters are inexpensive and easy to maintain. They are also effective and can be used to aerate the water

Internal view of an aerator. The rocker arm vibrates the diaphragm which, in turn, pumps out air via the nozzle at the front

Lighting Plants cannot survive without light. Yet, the excess light that an aquarium will receive if it is located near a window is likely to result in algal problems, at least, during the summer months. Sunlight is also unpredictable in many countries and is, obviously, impossible to control. Artificial lights, on the other hand, can be controlled quite easily. Their intensity, quality (wavelength) and the length of time they are switched on can all be manipulated to match the requirements of both plants and fish.

The range of aquarium lighting available today is quite extensive and includes, among others, tungsten bulbs, fluorescent tubes of various types which can emit light that will enhance plant growth or show up the colours of the fish, spotlights and high-pressure mercury bulbs. Of these, tungsten bulbs are the cheapest to install but not to run. At the opposite end of the scale, high-pressure mercury bulbs are expensive to install but cheap to run.

Every type of aquarium light also generates heat. Care must, therefore, be taken to ensure that no water splashes directly onto the bulb or tube. Many aquarium hoods have built-in protective measures such as condensation trays which lie between the lights and the water surface. If, however, the type of lighting chosen precludes the use of a hood (as is the case with spotlights and high-pressure mercury bulbs), the distance between these bulbs and the water surface must be at least 30 cm (12 in) to protect them against splashes, distribute the light adequately and minimise the risk of overheating the water surface.

It is probably more difficult to give advice on lighting than on any other single aspect of the home aquarium. So much depends on the quality of the light, the distance between the source and the surface of the water, the clarity of the water, the species of plants concerned, the density and design of the planting arrangements, and other factors, that any advice given for a particular situation may not apply fully to others.

A certain amount of experimentation is, therefore, almost always necessary. Any suggestions/instructions provided by manufacturers should, of course, be followed initially and adhered to or adjusted as developments dictate. In the case of tungsten bulbs and fluorescent tubes where the initial outlay is not particularly great, there is usually scope for several trial-and-error attempts in which the number and types of lights can be altered (possibly combining tungsten and fluorescent under one hood) until a pleasing and effective arrangement is arrived at.

As a rule, excessive light will result in an overabundance of unsightly green algal growth. Under illumination will encourage brown algae. In between lies a happy medium which may include the growth of some encrusting green algae on the rocks and sides of the aquarium. These rarely present a problem. The figures suggested in the table below should be taken as a working baseline for tungsten and fluorescent types of illumination. The resulting levels of light should be enough to prevent both types of algal problems mentioned while, at the same time, keeping most plants in a reasonable state of health.

Recommended Minimum Lighting Requirements

Approximate Aquarium Length		Wattage	
Inches	*Centimetres*	*Tungsten*	*Fluorescent*
18	45	1 × 40	1 × 8
24	60	2 × 40	1 × 15
36	90	3 × 40	2 × 20
48	120	3 × 60	2 × 30
60	150	5 × 40	2 × 40

Aeration One of the essential requirements of all aquaria is a plentiful supply of dissolved oxygen. Plants can produce some or most of this under certain conditions. However, the amount generated will fluctuate over a 24-hour period as photosynthesis 'switches on and off' in step with the light/dark period. For a reliable, steady supply, other methods must, therefore, be employed.

The most popular piece of equipment for this purpose is the diaphragm air pump, although other types are also widely available, e.g. piston or centrifugal (submerged) pumps. Irrespective of their mechanical or electrical design, all pumps have one thing in common – they cause agitation of the water surface. Diaphragm and piston pumps do this by having their air streams directed through diffusers (air stones) via a length of airline. As the air passes through the diffuser, it is broken up into small bubbles. These create a water current as they rise to the surface, thus bringing a continual supply of water molecules into direct contact with the atmosphere at the air/water interface. It is this that causes aeration, rather than the air contained in the bubbles themselves. In fact, very little oxygen can dissolve from a single bubble in the second or so that it takes for it to emerge from the diffuser, rise to the surface of the water and burst. The actual amount can be increased by reducing the overall size of each bubble, thereby increasing the total surface area available, or by producing curtains of bubbles, rather than a narrow stream.

An alternative method of reducing the size of bubbles is provided by non-electrical/mechanical aerators which rely on the dissociation of hydrogen peroxide into water and oxygen, the tiny bubbles passing into the water through the ceramic walls of the container in which the reaction takes place.

Submerged pumps create water turbulence whose aerating properties can often be enhanced through the incorporation of a spray-bar attachment which raises the current above the surface of the aquarium water and returns it via a series of fine jets. These agitate the surface and, therefore, enable exchange of gases to take place. Spray-bar attachments can also be linked to certain types of power filter, thus allowing aeration and filtration to be carried out with a single piece of equipment. Air streams produced by diaphragm and piston pumps can also be linked to filters of the box, sponge/foam, or undergravel types.

Filtration In the wild, toxic waste products do not usually present any problems since water currents and well-established bacterial populations render these compounds safe, either through dilution or biological breakdown, virtually as soon and as fast as they are generated.

In aquaria, this does not normally apply. Filters of various types are, therefore, employed to maintain toxic compounds and excessive debris within tolerable limits:

Mechanical filtration removes solid pieces of debris (such as bits of dead or decaying vegetation) and faeces (droppings produced by fish or snails) by channelling the dirty water through a suitable medium, e.g. filter wool, foam or diatomaceous sand.

Chemical filtration removes toxic chemicals, like ammonia, through absorption by highly porous compounds. Aquarium charcoal and zeolite are two suitable media.

Biological filtration neutralises the toxic potential of ammonia and nitrites through the metabolic activities of *Nitrosomonas* and *Nitrobacter* bacteria respectively (see page 18 for further details). Organic molecules are also broken down by a further group collectively referred to as heterotrophic bacteria.

Although it is possible to install a filter that will function primarily in one or other of these ways, it is usually better and just as easy to combine two or all three methods. In fact, mechanical filters will function biologically if

they are allowed to run for a sufficiently long period between cleanouts. If, in addition, a filter is functioning biologically, it follows (by definition) that it is also acting as a chemical filter.

The most basic and, consequently, generally cheapest type of filter is the internal air-operated corner or box filter which is designed primarily as a mechanical and/or chemical filter. The most sophisticated and expensive types are the electrical power filters. These are available in a range of sizes, designs and prices to suit the needs of even the most demanding of aquarists. The accompanying chart incorporates some of the main characteristics and types to allow comparisons to be made.

Filtration Chart

Type of Filter	Main Types of Filtration	Method of Operation
Internal Box Filter	Mechanical and Chemical	Air
External Box Filter	Mechanical and Chemical	Air or Electricity
Internal Sponge/Foam Filter	Mechanical and Biological	Air
Undergravel Filter (Normal and Reverse-flow)	Mechanical and Biological	Air or Electricity
Internal Power (Canister-type) Filter	Mechanical and Biological	Electricity
External Power (Canister-type) Filter	Mechanical, Chemical and Biological	Electricity
Diatom Filter	Mechanical	Electricity
Trickle-feed (Gravity) Water Purifiers/Filters	Mechanical and Biological	Air

Air-operated filters do not generate as much power as electrically operated ones. As a result, their turnover rate is considerably slower. Although this may be a disadvantage when fast, mechanical filtration is required, it is usually perfectly adequate for biological filtration purposes. In fact, a very fast turnover rate may not necessarily result in more effective biological filtration since bacteria, no matter how efficient they may be at processing ammonia and nitrites, have metabolic thresholds beyond which they cannot function.

Therefore, while power filters operate quite effectively at turnover rates of between one and three times the capacity of the tank per hour, undergravel biological filters can do their water purifying job quite satisfactorily at, perhaps, one complete exchange per hour or less. For fast, mechanical removal of really fine suspended particles, such as those which make water cloudy or milky, diatom filters are hard to beat.

As each type of filter has its own characteristics, it is impossible to say categorically which is the best since efficiency can only be measured in terms of the job done. Some mechanical filters may be more expensive than some biological ones but may not be the best choice if the latter type of filtration is desired. The opposite, of course, also applies. It is this consideration that should be foremost in the aquarist's mind when (s)he is in the process of choosing a filter.

Water Chemistry Water is a chemical compound made up of hydrogen (H) and oxygen (O) bonded together in the ratio of two hydrogen ions to every oxygen ion and represented in chemical shorthand by the formula H_2O. Despite its relatively simple composition, water is a remarkable substance. It is vital for the survival of every living thing and can account, in some cases, for as much as 90 per cent of the total body weight of an organism. It is also capable of reacting with virtually every other chemical substance known on earth,

though some reactions may be so slow as to be only detectable over long periods of time.

Because of its reactivity, water usually carries a large number of chemicals in solution. Several of these have already been mentioned elsewhere and their beneficial/detrimental effects have been discussed (metallic ions, ammonia, nitrites, etc). Two aspects of water chemistry, however, warrant further treatment. These are water hardness and pH.

Water Hardness The subject of water hardness probably causes more confusion among aquarists than any other. The main reason for this is that there is no single universally accepted scale. Consequently, various figures can be given for the same level of hardness depending on which units are being used. Gradually, though, things appear to be moving towards the use of the 'parts per million' scale. If and when this becomes universal, life will be considerably easier for all concerned. However, for the moment, we have to cope with the existing differences in terminology and units of hardness. It may, therefore, prove helpful to see how these relate to each other.

Hardness is a quality given to water by the amount of salts (mainly of calcium and magnesium) present. If the concentration is high, the water is hard. At the other extreme, water with few dissolved salts is soft. Total hardness can be subdivided into:

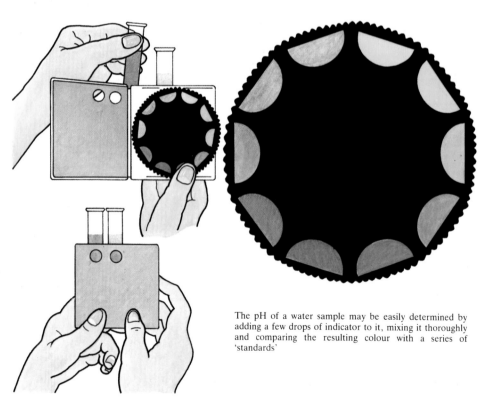

The pH of a water sample may be easily determined by adding a few drops of indicator to it, mixing it thoroughly and comparing the resulting colour with a series of 'standards'

(a) Carbonate, Bicarbonate or Temporary Hardness (KH) – the first of these names is misleading as this type of hardness is caused by the bicarbonates of calcium and magnesium. The last name is in recognition of the fact that Bicarbonate Hardness can be reduced or eliminated by boiling. This results in the formation of insoluble carbonates which are then deposited as scale or 'fur'.

(b) General or Permanent Hardness (GH). This cannot be eliminated or reduced by boiling.

Both types of hardness perform important roles in the lives of fish. Extremely low levels of Temporary Hardness, for example, can lead to abrupt changes in pH (see page 28) through lack of buffering capacity. These abrupt changes can result in serious imbalances in the fish, such as acidosis or alkalosis, or even death. Low levels of Permanent Hardness are required by species such as Discus (*Symphysodon* spp), while high levels must be provided for African Rift Lake Cichlids.

As far as units of measurement are concerned, these are calculated on the levels of certain calcium salts present in a given volume of water. Since both the salt itself and the volume differ between countries, this has given rise to a number of scales based on American, English (Clark) or German degrees of hardness.

For ease of reference, these may be converted to parts per million quite simply by using a conversion factor. The results can then be compared against a hardness chart:

American Degree × 17.1 = hardness in parts per million

English (Clark) Degree × 14.3 = hardness in parts per million

German Degree × 17.9 = hardness in parts per million

Water Hardness Chart

Hardness	Parts per million
Very soft	0–50
Moderately Soft	50–100
Slightly Hard	100–150
Moderately Hard	150–200
Hard	200–300
Very hard	Above 300

Establishing the correct hardness for a particular species is very important. Failure to do so can result in dietary deficiency diseases caused through the absence of certain mineral salts which are normally absorbed directly from the water (particularly if the food provided for these fish is also lacking in these compounds).

Damage to delicate gill tissues, inhibition of spawning behaviour, or a number of other problems can also occur.

Hardness of any sort can be reduced by dilution with rain or distilled water or through the addition of proprietary treatments. Temporary Hardness may be raised through the gradual addition of sodium bicarbonate. General Hardness can be increased by the inclusion of limestone or marble rocks in the tank or through the use of rinsed limestone/marble chippings, enclosed in a fine-meshed 'sock', as part of the water treatment medium in canister-type power filters. When this last approach is used, care must be taken to ensure that no small bits of rock enter the power filter impellor chamber. Were this to happen, the impellor could be seriously damaged. Proprietary treatments for raising the level of hardness are also available through aquatic retail shops. Finally, water hardness can be measured, and adjustments monitored, by means of accurate, inexpensive, easy-to-use test kits.

pH In the wild, fish are found in water which can range from extremely hard and alkaline to extremely soft and acid. Although these conditions may fluctuate seasonally or even daily, the magnitude of these fluctuations and the rate at which they take place will normally fall within the tolerance limits of the particular species concerned. Should deviations from the norm be too great or too abrupt, as in cases of acute pollution, considerable numbers of fish and other aquatic organisms will die.

On a less extreme level, inappropriate pH conditions will place fish under stress, thus opening them up to attack from pathogenic organisms. Relatively small fluctuations from the optimum can, however, be handled without too much difficulty. Many species, in fact, not only survive but also breed quite successfully within a range of pH values. Others, like Tiger Barbs (*Barbus tetrazona*), can survive in varying pH conditions but require soft acid water for the successful fertilisation of eggs. Adult pairs may, therefore, go through the complete spawning ritual in a tank having hardish alkaline water but will only manage a very low success rate in terms of egg fertilisation. Clearly, pH plays a very fundamental role. Yet, the factors that 'cause pH' are very uncomplicated indeed.

As mentioned earlier, water is a simple compound, represented chemically by the formula H_2O. If a molecule of water were to be split up, this would result in a positively charged hydrogen atom and a negatively charged hydroxyl molecule. Electrically charged particles such as these are called ions. It is the attraction between the positive hydrogen ion (H^+) and the negative hydroxyl ion (OH^-) that bonds them together into a neutral H_2O molecule. In pure water, the number of H^+ and OH^- ions are equal and balance each other out. Such water is said to be neutral with a pH value of 7.

However, water is not usually pure. It will, therefore, show an overabundance of either H^+ or OH^- ions. If there is an excess of H^+ ions, the water will be acidic with values below pH 7 (the lower the figure, the higher the acidity). If, on the other hand, there is an excess of OH^- ions, the water is said to be alkaline (the higher the figure, the higher the alkalinity). The scale itself runs from 0 to 14, strong acids having values around 1 and strong alkalis being represented by pH values between 13 and 14.

As a rule, tropical aquarium fish like water that is more or less neutral, i.e. pH 6.5 to 7.5. Some species will, of course, have very definite preferences or requirements and these will have to be met. It is not just the actual pH value that is important, but also the rate at which changes are allowed to occur. If these are too abrupt, fish will suffer or die even though the original and resulting values may both be within the range normally indicated for a species. The main reason for this is that the pH scale is not a linear one like most others – it is logarithmic. In effect, what this means is that the intervals between units represent differences that increase by a factor of 10 each time. For example, a pH value of 5 indicates a level of acidity which is lower than that represented by pH 6 by a factor 10 times lower than that represented by a pH value of 7. Looked at in a different way, a water sample having a pH of 5 would require 10 times more neutralising agent than one having a pH of 6.

It is only when the significance of the pH scale is fully appreciated that the profound effect of what, at first sight, appear to be minor fluctuations can be seen in their real light. Should changes in pH be necessary, these can be carried out quite easily. The level of acidity may be increased by using peat plates under the gravel or peat fibre (enclosed in a fine-meshed 'sock') as part of a power filter sandwich. Alternatively, the sock may be suspended inside the tank and left there to do its job. If none of these methods is possible or desirable, water can be acidified in a bucket by adding about a handful of washed, rinsed peat per gallon and allowing this to stand until the required pH is obtained. Raising the pH is even simpler. Limestone or marble rocks or chippings, used as recommended in the preceding section on Water Hardness, should soon bring about measurable changes.

For those aquarists who prefer an even easier method, there are inexpensive commercially produced pH adjusters. When altering pH levels, frequent monitoring with a pH Test Kit is necessary to avoid potential disasters. Even if no adjustments are necessary, the regular use of a kit is strongly recommended.

Aquarium Accessories Adequate heating, lighting, aeration, filtration and water chemistry are, obviously, of paramount importance for the successful maintenance of tropical aquaria. It would be a mistake, though, to think that they alone will be sufficient to meet all requirements and situations. Attention must, in addition, be paid to other equipment – those bits and pieces which are collectively known as 'accessories'.

Some are very obvious and distinctly aquatic. Nets of various sizes and coarseness (one per tank), spare heater-stats wired up and ready for use at a moment's notice and algae scrapers are just three such accessories. Others have no immediate aquatic connection but are just as useful. Suitable examples of this type of accessory are long forceps (for planting or removal of dead fish), jam jars (for fish introductions), an electrical screwdriver, insulating/waterproof tape and spare fuses.

The following list may be found useful in gathering together a range of accessories which will help in the smooth running of aquaria.

Aquarium Accessories List

Item	Some Uses
Spare inexpensive aerator	Temporary replacement in case of breakdown, particularly in aquaria with undergravel filtration.
Non-return airline valve	Will prevent water siphoning back into aerator when/if this is switched off.
T and Y pieces	Make a variety of airline arrangements possible.
Airline	As addition to, or replacement for, existing arrangement or new aquaria.
Airline clips	Method of controlling rate of airflow through airlines.
Spare diffusers	Those in use can become clogged up under certain water conditions, may lose efficiency or may experience deterioration of the joint between airline and diffuser.

Spare diaphragm	Diaphragm in use may tear without warning. Prompt replacement is essential.
Range of fuses	In case of electrical malfunction, fuses in plugs may blow. The range kept in reserve should match that of the plugs in use.
Cable tidy	Method of keeping wiring neat and safe.
Insulating/ waterproof tape	Means of protecting electrical connections and aquarists(!).
Heater-stat clips	Replacement of those in use which can sometimes deteriorate after a time or break during routine maintenance.
Spare heater-stat fully wired up	Essential – may never be required but if/when it is, its value becomes self-evident.
Thermometer	If spirit models are used, these can easily break. If liquid crystal, adhesive ones are used, these cannot usually be reused if peeled off. In either case, replacements are necessary.
Range of nets	Should include small, fine nets for transferring/catching fry, and young fish; large fine ones for delicate species and coarser ones in a variety of sizes for more robust species.
Breeding trap	Method of confining/protecting a pregnant livebearing female and her fry during birth and until appropriate accommodation for the young can be made available. All models provide means of keeping the female (which will often eat her offspring) and the fry apart.
Jam jars	Useful for transferring adult fish and fry, as very temporary quarters for fry, as treatment chambers and a multitude of other useful functions.
Pair of long forceps	Useful for removing dead fish, plants and objects from an aquarium. Can double up as planting stick.
Planting sticks	Self-explanatory.
Waterproof marker pen	Writing details of species, treatments administered, spawnings, etc on tanks.
Algae cleaner/ scraper	Means of keeping sides of tanks free of encrusting algae. Magnetic cleaners allow the job to be done without getting one's hands wet.
Siphon tube	Used for water changes. Tube should be at least as long as the distance between the rim of the tank and the floor, plus the height/depth of the tank.
Gravel cleaner/ dip tube	Useful for cleaning localised accumulations of debris or uneaten food which do not require a partial/major water change.
Screwdrivers	Standard and star-tipped types should be kept handy for wiring up plugs and maintaining/cleaning/stripping down electrical equipment (as long as the aquarist is familiar with correct methods of coping with electricity!).
Scissors	Useful for cutting airlines, insulating/waterproof tape, etc.
Water testing kits	Essential for monitoring and adjusting water chemistry.
pH adjusters	Useful, quick methods of altering acid/base balance of the water to suit particular species.
Medicine chest with remedies for common diseases	Should be regarded as an essential safeguard but should not be resorted to as a matter of habit. Prevention is better than cure.
Small reserve stock of food	Useful means of overcoming oversights, particularly at weekends.
Worm feeding ring	Keeps Tubifex confined to a relatively small area and minimises risks of widespread distribution of uneaten worms.
Tube of silicone-based sealant	Emergency repair of leaks. Useful for attaching bark/bogwood to plastic/glass plates which can then be covered with gravel to prevent them from floating.

Setting up a Tropical Aquarium

Setting up an aquarium is not merely a question of obtaining all the necessary equipment, gravel/rooting medium, fish, plants, foods and remedies, taking them home and putting the lot together in the space of a few hours. Many have tried this – and many have failed. Patience is a quality that every aquarist should cultivate. There is no substitute for a thoroughly pre-planned, patient approach.

Ideally, the first step should consist of background reading and discussions with an experienced aquarist. This aquarist could, of course, be the owner of the shop from which the aquarium set-up will eventually be bought. Early decisions should then be taken on, at least, the following:

1. Size of the aquarium – the larger the better.
2. Type of aquarium – community species, single species, related types, etc.
3. Filtration – e.g. undergravel or power filtration.
4. Aeration – e.g. will it be supplied by an air pump or a power filter spray-bar attachment?

5. Lighting – tungsten bulbs, fluorescent tubes, spotlights or high-pressure mercury bulbs?
6. Plants – are they compatible with the fish? Some Cichlids, for example, will regularly uproot plants.
7. Expense – are there sufficient funds to cover the envisaged set-up? If not, it is best to start again from scratch – a modestly priced but well-equipped aquarium is far superior to an expensive, under-equipped one.

Once these aspects have been investigated and some informed opinions have been taken, a further set of issues should be tackled. These should include decisions on:

1. Appropriate stocking levels of fish and plants.
2. Amount and types of aquarium decor.
3. Amount and types of rooting media.

Fish Stocking Levels The understandable and unavoidable temptation that every new aquarist experiences on starting up in the hobby is to fill a tank up with the maximum possible number of fish from the outset. Should the temptation prove too strong, disappointment will almost certainly follow, often within the first few days.

There are many reasons for this, two important ones being:

1. A new tank is too raw to handle a full complement of fish as efficiently as a mature, established one (although modern-day water conditioners help considerably).
2. The development of aquatic skills requires a little time.

A sensible approach is to set up a tank with all systems running, condition the water and allow a week to elapse before introducing 50 per cent of the eventual stocks of fish. The remaining 50 per cent should then be added gradually as the tank settles down and matures.

Stocking levels are quite easy to estimate. However, the figures obtained should be regarded as guidelines only – they are not foolproof, inflexible rules. The only real rule as far as numbers are concerned is that overstocking must be avoided at all costs. The distressing problems that go hand in hand with an overcrowded tank, such as excessive aggression, deterioration in water quality, loss of condition in the fish and outbreaks of disease, are all preventable if a reasonable approach is taken. In addition, overstocking is unfair on the tank occupants themselves.

The main factor to be considered when working out stocking levels is the surface area of water available. The reason for this is that the number of fish that an aquarium can hold is determined by the amount of oxygen present in solution. As explained elsewhere, most of the oxygen dissolves into the water at the surface. Volume does have a part to play in that, the larger it is, the greater is its capacity to resist abrupt changes, but when it comes to stocking levels, its role is secondary.

Fish vary a great deal in size, level of activity, dietary requirements, behaviour, oxygen requirements and a host of other parameters. This makes it impossible to provide a universally applicable stocking level formula. The details given here are designed to apply to relatively peaceful herbivores/omnivores. In the case of aggressive carnivores/piscivores (which, incidentally, produce higher quantities of water-polluting wastes), reductions in the recommended levels will be necessary.

By starting off at 50 per cent stocking level, as recommended for a new tank, many problems can be avoided. It is always easier to add than to remove fish. A workable rule-of-thumb would be:

1. For small species, e.g. Neons (*Paracheirodon innesi*), the approximate number is arrived at by dividing the surface area in square centimetres by 80 (square inches by 13).
2. For medium-sized fish, i.e. between 5 and 7.5 cm (2–3 in), the conversion factors are 104 (cm) and 18 (in) respectively.
3. For larger fish, measuring between 7.5 and 10 cm (3–4 in), the figures are 133 (cm) and 20 (in).

In all these calculations, the length of the tail (caudal fin) is ignored. This is very important – if the tail were included, a Swordtail (*Xiphophorus helleri*) with a body length of 5 cm (2 in), could easily and wrongly end up in category 3 instead of category 2 or (even) 1.

Using the conversion factors given above, a chart of approximate recommended stocking levels can be established:

Plant stocking levels Plants add a special dimension to an aquarium. On the aesthetic side, colourful, imaginative displays can be created both with living and artificial plants (some of which are very effective). On the biological side, living plants have the added qualities of acting as buffering agents and natural water purifiers. However, even in those aquaria where living plants cannot be used owing to the activities of the fish – for example, Oscars (*Astronotus ocellatus*) and living plants are not comfortable tankmates – the inclusion of weighted artificial plants can afford shelter and, thus, help to reduce stress.

Approximate Recommended Stocking Levels

Aquarium Surface Dimensions		Number of Fish		
Inches	Centimetres (Approx.)	Up to 5 cm (2 in)	5–7.5 cm (2–3 in)	7.5–10 cm (3–4 in)
18 × 10	45 × 25	14	10	Not Recommended
24 × 12	60 × 30	22	16	14
36 × 12	90 × 30	33	24	21
48 × 12	120 × 30	44	32	29
60 × 18	150 × 45	83	60	54

Common Name	Scientific Name	Comments
Guppy	*Poecilia reticulata*	Numerous fancy varieties are available
Swordtail Platy	*Xiphophorus helleri* *Xiphophorus maculatus* *Xiphophorus variatus*	These species are very closely related and inter-breed. Male Swordtails can be aggressive towards each other
Molly	*Poecilia sphenops* *Poecilia latipinna* *Poecilia velifera*	All Mollies should be kept in water containing about one teaspoonful of salt per gallon
Zebra Danio	*Brachydanio rerio*	This is a very fast swimming shoaler
Spotted Danio	*Brachydanio nigrofasciatus*	This species is similar to its close relative, the Zebra
Neon Cardinal	*Paracheirodon innesi* *Paracheirodon axelrodi*	These two species are very similar to each other. Cardinals have more colour. Both are shoalers
Harlequin	*Rasbora heteromorpha*	A beautiful shoaling species with a cone-shaped dark patch in the posterior half of the body
Tiger Barb	*Barbus tetrazona*	Lively shoaling species. May nip fins. Several varieties are available
Angel	*Pterophyllum scalare*	Only small specimens should be kept in a community tank. Several varieties are available
Bronze Catfish	*Corydoras aeneus*	This species is also available in an albino form. Good, sturdy bottom-level feeder
Kuhli Loach	*Acanthophthalmus semicinctus*	This is a peaceful eel-like species
Sucking Loach/ Chinese Algae Eater	*Gyrinocheilus aymonieri*	Sucker-mouthed very fast-swimming herbivore. Some specimens can be aggressive
Plecostomus	*Hypostomus* spp	Sucker-mouthed herbivore. More peaceful than the Sucking Loach and a slower mover
Dwarf Gourami Three-spot/Blue/ Gold/Platinum/ Cosby/Opaline Gourami	*Colisa lalia* *Trichogaster trichopterus*	These species have special air-breathing organs. *T. trichopterus* males can be aggressive
Siamese Fighter	*Betta splendens*	Only single males may be kept safely in a community aquarium

Since many plants can grow to great lengths and may require regular pruning, terms such as 'small' must be regarded as relative in the guidelines given below, i.e. it is quite possible to have a small *Cabomba* plant simply by snipping a short piece of stem from an established plant measuring over 30 cm (12 in) in length.

Genuinely small plants are represented by species such as Hair Grass (*Eleocharis acicularis*) whose fine filamentous leaves can grow up to 20 cm (8 in) but are generally considerably shorter, or *Sagittaria subulata* (forma *pusilla*) which does not normally exceed 10 cm (4 in) in height. Whatever type of small plant is chosen, the recommended stocking level is around 50 plants per square foot (*c* 900 sq cm). For medium-sized plants, the concentration will, obviously, be lower (perhaps 20 to 25). In the case of substantial plants like the larger Amazon Swords (*Echinodorus* spp), single, or just a few, specimens are usually enough.

Aquarium decorations The choice of tank decor depends on a number of factors which include personal taste on the one hand and the needs of the fish on the other. Ceramic divers, frogs, bridges, sunken galleons and the like are, clearly, concerned with personal taste. Some may incidentally provide shelter or a suitable spawning site but their primary aims are purely decorative. Printed aquarium backgrounds, usually featuring underwater scenes which can be stuck on to the external surface of the back of an aquarium, also fall into this category.

Natural, or natural-looking synthetic items, are more versatile in that they are not only decorative but are also meant to act as terracing, refuges or spawning sites. Bogwood, driftwood, bark, mangrove roots, simulated wood, pieces of slate, other types of natural rock and simulated rock are all widely available. Natural woods may already be pre-treated at the time of purchase and may not, therefore, require further processing. If this is not the case, they need to be soaked in water for a prolonged period (this can take several weeks) to minimise their water-staining properties or to leach out excess salt (in the case of driftwood). If the pieces are allowed to dry out thoroughly after soaking, they can then be painted with non-toxic clear varnish to prevent or at least reduce further staining.

Non-reactive rocks such as slate can be used without fear of altering the chemical properties of the water. However, limestone, marble and other calcite-bearing rocks will raise the alkalinity of the water over a period of time.

Clearly, such rocks are ideal for aquaria housing species which require or prefer such conditions. Despite their pH-raising qualities, these rocks can also be used in many community aquaria as long as a close check is kept on conditions with pH test kit and regular partial water changes are carried out (this should be done anyway).

Rooting Media A common misconception which, happily, is gradually being rectified, is that the nature of the rooting medium is relatively unimportant in aquaria. One possible contributory factor to this myth is the fact that submerged aquatic plants can absorb some of the nutrients they require for healthy growth through their leaves. In the case of rootless plants, such as the Hornworts (*Ceratophyllum* spp), all nutrients, other than those formed during photosynthesis, enter the plant via the leaves.

Most plants, however, possess roots. In floating species, these are usually suspended in the water. If conditions are sufficiently shallow, though, the roots will grow into the substratum and anchor the plants just as they do in submerged species. In addition to anchorage, roots also provide plants with the means of absorbing nutrients from the surrounding medium. The nature of this medium is, therefore, of extreme importance and careful thought given to this aspect of aquarium management will pay off handsomely.

Gravel is inexpensive, clean, always available and easy to handle. Not surprisingly, it is the most popular aquarium bedding medium used. Most shops will stock, at least, two different grain sizes as well as a selection of artificial (often coloured) gravels. Despite its many advantages, aquarium gravel is, initially, sterile. Submerged plants which absorb significant amounts of nutrients through their roots will, therefore, find gravel only suitable as a means of anchorage unless adequate steps are taken. Liquid, crystal, pelleted and other types of aquarium plant food will all help under such circumstances. This treatment should continue at least until the micro-organisms which render gravel biologically active have developed and some mulm (organic debris) has sunk into the inter-granular spaces.

Even when this process has been completed, many plants will require further assistance. This can be provided by means of water treatments like carbon dioxide diffusers (to aid photosynthesis) or by careful choice of additional/alternative rooting media such as peat plates, 'plugs' for individual plants, mini peat/loam bags or plants grown in containers.

Two basic questions need to be asked when deciding on the choice of rooting medium:
1. Which medium is best for the chosen plants?
2. Is this compatible with the chosen species?

As a rule, plants which have deep penetrating roots require a largish grain size which should be, at least, that of very coarse sand. Shallow-rooted plants and those that have a tendency to float can best be anchored in media having a finer grain. In the latter case, under-gravel filter plates could become blocked if the grain size is too fine. A balance is obviously necessary aided, perhaps, by the use of a gravel 'tidy' which can be laid on the filter to prevent such blockages occurring.

Peat plates, while being excellent for many plants, will be unsuitable in aquaria housing fish species which prefer or require alkaline conditions. They are equally unsuitable in aquaria whose bottom layers are continually being disturbed through the activities of the fish. The most obvious activity of this type is digging, common among Cichlids, such as mouthbrooders or the various *Geophagus* species (the name actually translates as 'earth eater'). Other fish disrupt the substratum by burrowing. The best-known examples of this type are the Coolie or Kuhli Loaches (*Acanthophthalmus* spp) and the Spiny Eels (*Macrognathus* and *Mastacembelus* spp), which, incidentally, are not true eels. If such species are to be kept successfully, the nature of the bedding medium needs to be sufficiently fine to allow them to burrow without injuring themselves in the process. Coarse media, such as gravel, are not, therefore, suitable for these fish.

Whatever medium is used, the amount must be sufficient for the plant roots to establish themselves properly. Roughly speaking, the depth of medium should be at least 5 cm (2 in). If undergravel filters are incorporated into the system, it may be desirable to increase this to a minimum of 7.5 cm (3 in). The shallowest area should be at the front or side to allow easy access for the removal of excess debris from time to time.

With a little thought to rooting/bedding media, plants and fish can both be kept satisfactorily in an attractive, balanced environment. Failure to plan this aspect of setting up can, however, result in an aquarium that is not just unsightly but also unsuitable for the plants, the fish, the aquarist, or all three.

Setting up – Step by Step Guide As the foregoing paragraphs will have shown, setting up a tropical aquarium must not be allowed to be a hit-and-miss affair. It is far better to decide to become an aquarist and follow this with planning, than to take up the hobby and buy everything on impulse.

If the former option has been adopted and the points discussed earlier have been considered, the next major step is to obtain all the necessary equipment and plants, *but not the fish* (these should come later).

Setting up procedures vary according to circumstances, equipment selected, experience and opinion. The following is just one approach. It is designed to help first-time aquarists avoid major pitfalls and could form the basis for refinements and adjustments as individual conditions dictate.

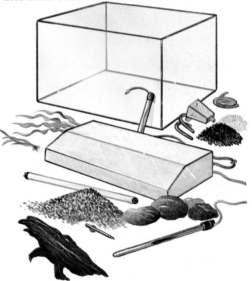

Aquarium equipment: phase 1

Phase 1
Check that all the necessary equipment has been bought:

Aquarium, stand (if necessary), hood (unnecessary if spotlights or mercury bulbs have been chosen), condensation tray, lights, starter unit (if lights are fluorescent), heater-stat, thermometer, aerator, airline, non-return valve, diffuser stone, filter, filter media (if model is not of the undergravel type), gravel, terracing/rocks/wood, plants (to be kept moist), plugs (one for each piece of electrical equipment – if a cable tidy is used, only one plug may be necessary), water testing kits.

NB Accessory equipment, such as algae scrapers and nets, will need to be bought soon but are not absolutely essential on Day 1.

Phase 2
1. Choose appropriate position for the aquarium – away from direct sunlight, draughts and extremes of temperature.

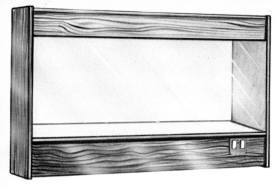
Strong aquarium stand: phase 2

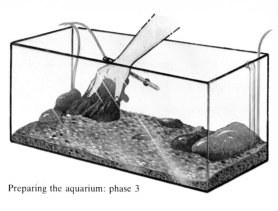
Preparing the aquarium: phase 3

2. Check on sturdiness of cupboard or other cabinet if the aquarium is to be placed on household furniture. Aquarium cabinets and stands are specially designed to support the considerable weight represented by a fully furnished aquarium. For example, a 60 × 30 × 30 cm (24 × 12 × 12 in) aquarium will hold about 54.6 kg (120 lb) of water. Water weighs a great deal: each Imperial gallon (1.2 US gallons) weighs about 4.5 kg (10 lb). In metric equivalents, 1 litre of water weighs 1 kg (2.2 lb). Gravel weighs approximately 100 lb per cu ft (c 45.4 kg per 0.028 cu metre); rocks weigh half as much again. Finally, the weight of the glass, hood, lighting units, etc, will add a further few kilograms to the total.

3. Rinse aquarium thoroughly to remove dust and dirt.

4. Fill aquarium and test for leaks.

5. Drain completely. If there is a leak, repair it with silicone sealant.

6. Lay polystyrene sheet (or equivalent) on the aquarium stand or cabinet and rest the aquarium on it. The polystyrene will mould itself around any irregularities present, thus cushioning the base of the aquarium and protecting it against fracturing.

Phase 3
1. Place undergravel filter into position if one is being used.

2. Lay gravel tidy on top of the filter plates if one is being used.

3. Rinse gravel/sand thoroughly – until water runs clear.

4. Spread a layer of gravel/sand on the filter plate or gravel tidy.

5. Add layer or pockets of organic planting medium if required.

6. Add remainder of gravel/sand and arrange aquascape with chosen rocks, bogwood, etc. Generally speaking, the lowest terraces should be at the front and the highest at the back.

Personal taste plays an important part here but, if possible, symmetrical arrangements should be avoided.

7. Place heater, thermostat, airline and internal filters in their permanent positions. These, plus undergravel filter airlifts, can all be hidden from view by careful arrangement of rocks, etc. Ensure that the heater does not touch the gravel or lies directly against any object. *NB Do not switch anything on!*

Filling with water: phase 4

Phase 4
1. Start filling aquarium with water. Avoid disturbing the bedding medium by pouring the water onto a sheet of newspaper, greaseproof paper or plastic laid over the aquascape. Alternatively, pour the water into a jar or jug placed on a saucer. The important thing is to avoid direct contact between the stream of water and the bedding medium.

2. Fill aquarium up to the halfway mark only.

3. Add a small quantity of warm water to raise the temperature into the tropical range (even plants can feel the cold!).

4. Remove newspaper, jars, etc.

5. Introduce the plants, ensuring that small species are placed near the front. Make sure

that plants whose leaves emerge from a crown, e.g. *Vallisneria* and Amazon Swords, have this part exposed. If covered, crowns can rot.

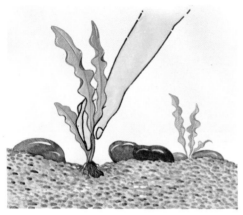

Positioning planting: phase 4

6. Add water conditioners and dechlorinator.

7. Complete filling process leaving at least 2.5 cm (*c* 1 in) between the surface of the water and the edge of the glass.

8. Arrange power filter inflow/outflow tubes or push powerhead into position on top of the undergravel filter airlift. (This step will obviously depend on the filtration system being used.)

9. Lower condensation tray into position.

10. Install lights in hood.

11. Place hood in its permanent position.

12. Arrange cables, airline, starter unit, etc, in hood compartment if this is available. If not, arrange leads and airline neatly out of view behind the aquarium. If cable tidy is being used, wiring can be completed at this stage.
NB Take great care to keep all connections dry!

13. Insert non-return valve in the airline.

14. Locate aerator above tank level, e.g. suspended from a hook on the wall.

15. Set up power filter connections.

Phase 5
1. Switch on all electrical equipment. This should be done, preferably, in the morning to allow for monitoring and adjustments.

2. Adjust air and filter flow rates – neither should be too turbulent.

3. Check temperature hourly and adjust thermostat if necessary.

NB (i) Switch off all electrical appliances before any adjustments are made.
(ii) Allow heater to cool down for about ten minutes before removing it from the water.

4. Test pH and hardness and adjust if necessary (see earlier sections on these topics).

5. Run the system on a 12–15 hour light period for a week if possible. Leave heater-stat, aeration and filter systems permanently switched on. This week-long period is not an absolute necessity with the water treatments and conditioners available today. However, it is advisable since it allows the aquarium to settle down and the aquarist to carry out adjustments and generally become familiar with the art of aquarium management.

During the first week, the water may become cloudy – this is quite normal and is caused by a 'bloom' of micro-organisms. It should clear within a few days, marking the end of the first major observable stage in the maturing process.

Phase 6
1. Work out the stocking level of fish for your tank.

2. Select compatible species, e.g. avoid aggressive or overlarge specimens. (Check under individiual species for relevant details.)

3. Obtain only about 50 per cent of your eventual stocks at the outset.

4. Select fish which are lively and well coloured, hold their fins erect, are full-bodied and are known to be feeding in the shop. If buying shoaling species, such as Neons, Cardinal Tetras or Zebra Danios, obtain at least six specimens. There are numerous species available for community aquaria. These are usually referred to as 'community species'. The accompanying list features some of the most common and may be used as the basis for the first shopping list:

5. If possible, arrange to buy your fish in the late afternoon to allow for an evening introduction. This will give the fish time to adjust to their new surroundings (see Phase 7 below).

6. Minimise heat loss by ensuring that fish are packed in a heat-resistant bag, such as those used to keep take-away food warm. Failing this, the bags containing the fish may be wrapped in newspaper or other insulating material. Avoid carrying exposed bags of fish – they are under enough stress already and can do without being subjected to this added ordeal.

Fish transporter: phase 6

7. Get the fish home as quickly as possible.

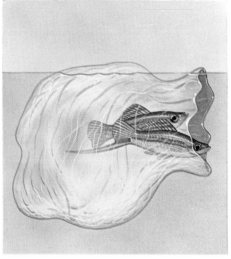

Releasing fish: phase 7

Phase 7

1. On getting home, switch off the aquarium lights.

2. Float the bags containing the fish in the aquarium.

3. Leave for about ten minutes to allow temperatures to equilibrate. Individual bags may require a longer period if they contain a large volume of water.

4. Untie the bags.

5. Replace about a quarter of the water in each bag with aquarium water.

6. Leave for ten minutes.

7. Repeat steps 5 and 6 twice more. (This introduces the fish to their new water chemistry gradually and helps reduce environmental shock.)

8. Gently release the fish into the aquarium.

9. Leave aquarium lights switched off.

10. Do not feed fish for several hours at least (preferably not until the following morning).

NB If Phase 7 is carried out during the late afternoon or early evening, this allows the fish time to become accustomed to their new surroundings in naturally fading light. They will, therefore, be able to explore the aquarium and find suitable shelters for the night without the need to do so in the full glare of the aquarium lights. They should also be allowed to see their first day in with naturally increasing daylight.

Tubifex worm feeder: phase 8

Phase 8

1. Keep a close check on all fish for signs of discomfort, injury or disease. Treat affected fish either in a separate quarantine tank (see page 45) or in the community aquarium.

2. Feed the fish sparingly but regularly – two or three small feeds per day are preferable to a single large one. Remove any uneaten food that remains after about five minutes.

3. Carry out regular tests on water quality and adjust conditions *gradually* if necessary.

Fish quarantine tank: phase 9

Phase 9

1. Set up quarantine tank (see page 45) and allow to mature in the normal way.

2. Obtain remaining 50 per cent of stock of fish using the same criteria outlined in Phase 6.

3. Subject the new fish to a period of acclimatisation as described under quarantine.

Phase 10

1. Transfer quarantined stock to main aquarium following guidelines supplied in Phase 7.

2. Keep a close check on things and take remedial action if necessary, e.g. removal of harassed or excessively aggressive individuals to quarantine tank. Exchanges of such fish can sometimes be arranged with other aquarists or with the shop which supplied the stock and equipment.

NB Completion of Phase 10 marks the end of the 'setting up period' and the beginning of the 'regular aquarium management period'.

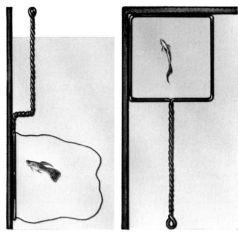

Nets for catching fish: phase 10

Tropical Aquarium Management

Just as setting up procedures vary according to circumstances or opinion, so do aquarium management routines. The following suggested approach should, at least, prevent major oversights, particularly during the first few months following the setting up period described above.

Daily

1. Feed fish, at least twice.

2. Check on state of health of fish and remove affected individuals for treatment if necessary.

3. Check for signs of breeding activity and remove fry or courting fish to appropriate quarters.

4. Check water temperature.

5. Switch aquarium lights on several minutes after the room lights have been on or after daybreak.

6. Check on state of health of nocturnal and/or crepuscular (twilight) species in the evening and provide food for them just before or just after lights out.

7. Switch aquarium lights off several minutes before the room lights are switched off or shortly before natural daylight fades.

Weekly

1. Do not feed the fish for a day (this does not apply either to fish being conditioned for spawning or to fry and juveniles).

2. Check heaters and thermostats for signs of faults, e.g. leakages.

3. Check pH, hardness and nitrite levels and take remedial action if necessary – ensure that changes are made gradually.

4. Check on supplies of food, water treatments and remedies.

Fortnightly

1. Switch off aeration.

2. Rake or otherwise stir up (gently!) the surface of the bedding medium.

3. Scrape excess algal growth from the front of the aquarium.

4. Allow debris to settle.

5. Siphon off debris along with 20–25 per cent of the aquarium water.

6. Replace this with fresh water whose temperature, pH and hardness match conditions in the aquarium. If a larger volume of water is being replaced, the fresh water must be treated with a dechlorinator and/or dechloraminator.

7. Switch on aeration.

NB These regular partial water changes should not be carried out in the morning unless the tap has been allowed to run for several minutes to eliminate toxic metallic ions, e.g. copper.

Three-weekly/Monthly

1. a) Clean out/replace non-biological filter media in sponge/foam, canister-type or box filters.

b) Rinse biological filter media in sponge/foam, canister-type or box filters.

NB Do not sterilise or boil biological media – this will destroy their microfauna and, consequently, make them ineffective until a new population is established.

2. If undergravel filtration is used, remove airline from airlift and scrape off any algal or calcite (hardwater) deposits from the opening.

3. Introduce siphon tube down each undergravel filter airlift and suck out a small amount of accumulated mulm (organic debris).

4. Clean or scrape diffuser stones.

5. Check aerator diaphragms.

6. Clean airline non-return valve.

7. Clean condensation tray or cover glass.

8. Check lighting equipment, e.g. terminals.

9. Remove dead and dying leaves from plants.

10. Prune, thin out and generally tidy up vegetation.

11. Replace poor plant specimens.

If Things Go Wrong

No matter how much time and care is devoted to an aquarium, things will go wrong from time to time. For example, equipment may fail, the fish may behave abnormally (or exhibit disease symptoms) or excessive growth of algae may develop.

Some Courses of Action 1. In the case of disease symptoms, these should be checked against the charts provided earlier under Fish Health (see page 27) and appropriate corrective measures taken.

2. If the fish behave abnormally without obvious symptoms of disease, carry out a complete check on the water conditions and the equipment. If these prove to be satisfactory, then carry out a partial water change and check the behaviour against the lists of symptoms which appear in the disease charts referred to in 1 (above).

NB Switch off electricity supply before handling any electrical equipment.

3. In the event of equipment failure, a good selection of accessories may well provide the necessary solution (see Aquarium Accessories List on page 62). If a major piece of equipment like a power filter, lighting starter unit or aerator fails, several hours (at least) will elapse

before the situation becomes critical unless, of course, the fault is such that it causes an electrical current to run through the aquarium water itself. In the case of undergravel filters operated by aerators, the bacteria will begin to suffer after a few hours if their air supply is cut off.

4. Excessive algal growth takes three forms:
a) Green water or green algae on plants, aquarium sides and ornaments. The cause is, almost invariably, too much light. Reducing the intensity or duration of the light, followed by a partial water change, physical removal of algal filaments and treatment with a proprietary aquarium algicide should remedy the problem.

b) Brown encrustations on plants, aquarium sides and ornaments, often accompanied by poor plant growth. Brown algae indicate insufficient illumination.

c) Blue-green algal 'mats' on plants, aquarium sides and ornaments indicate a high level of organic pollution. Physical removal of the mats, followed by a partial water change, a review of the aquarium maintenance routine with a view to preventing further accumulation of organic pollutants (e.g. too much food, inadequate filtration or aeration, overstocking, etc) and, finally, treatment with a proprietary algicide should eliminate this problem.

5. If fish appear unhappy/unwell during the first few weeks of an aquarium being set up, they may be regarded as suffering from the new tank syndrome. The most common causes of this are:

a) Excessively raw water.

b) Abrupt changes in water quality.

c) Improperly managed temperature adjustments.

d) Overstocking with fish.

e) Understocking with plants.

f) Overfeeding.

g) Incompatibility of species.

h) Inconsiderate transportation of fish.

i) Improperly managed introduction of fish into the aquarium.

j) Poor stocks of fish.

All these have been dealt with under various headings earlier.

Selection of Fish Species
for the
Tropical Aquarium

Setting the Scene

There are so many species of tropical fish currently kept by aquarists that any attempts at presenting a complete iisting is bound to fail or be out of date as soon as it is produced. For example, over 150 species and varieties of livebearers are maintained and bred in aquaria by specialist fishkeepers in the UK alone! The picture for Europe and the USA is not significantly different. Similarly, Cichlids, Killifish, Catfish, Anabantoids and many other types of fish all have their own dedicated following. If we add to this the large numbers of species kept by general aquarists, we can begin to appreciate the enormity/impossibility of the task facing anyone who attempts to cover the range comprehensively.

A selection, therefore, has to be made. By definition, this means that many species will have to be omitted in the name of practicability. Despite this limitation, the selection of fish presented in the following pages contains representative species of all the most common groups and families of fish kept in tropical freshwater aquaria.

Although every single species or variety is worthy of lengthy treatment, this (again) is out of the scope of a book such as this which emphasises the practical aspects of fishkeeping and the principles behind them. The details included for each fish are, therefore, those which are thought to be the most relevant when deciding which fish to choose either for the community or the single-species aquarium.

Livebearers

These fish are represented in tropical aquaria by species from five families: Poeciliidae, Anablepidae, Jenynsiidae, Goodeidae and Exocoetidae. Some differences in nomenclature may occur in the literature depending on which classification is adopted. The one included here follows traditional lines, but a new, proposed reclassification is also indicated, in brackets, in the descriptions that follow to allow for cross-reference should this new classification become widely adopted. It should be said here that some of the arguments appear very strong but acceptance (when it comes) invariably takes a long time. (See Parenti, L. R., in the Bibliography for fuller details).

Family Poeciliidae (Subfamily Poeciliinae)

COMMON NAMES: **Guppy, Millions Fish.**

SCIENTIFIC NAME: *Poecilia reticulata.*

SYNONYMS: *Lebistes reticulatus, Girardinus gupii.*

SIZE: Males up to 3 cm (1.2 in); females 6 cm (2.5 in).

RANGE: Wide distribution north of the Amazon. Introduced for control of malarial mosquitoes in many countries.

NATURAL HABITAT: Wide range of standing and gently flowing waters.

WATER CONDITIONS: Will tolerate wide range of conditions but prefers soft or slightly hard water with a teaspoonful of salt per gallon. Temperature: 21–26°c (70–79°F).

DIET: Will accept most foods.

NOTES: A peaceful, hardy species available in numerous colour and finnage varieties.

Guppy, female

COMMON NAME: **Swordtail**

SCIENTIFIC NAME: *Xiphophorus helleri.*

SYNONYM: None.

SIZE: Males (excluding sword) up to 10 cm (4 in); females 12 cm (4.7 in).

RANGE: Mexico (Atlantic Coast) and northern Central America.

NATURAL HABITAT: Wide range of (usually) clear, fast-moving waters.

WATER CONDITIONS: Slightly alkaline, medium hard water is preferred but will tolerate a range of conditions. Temperature around 24°c (75°F).

DIET: Will accept most foods.

NOTES: Males are often aggressive towards each other. Numerous colour and finnage varieties are available.

Guppy, male

Swordtail, male

COMMON NAME:	**Platy.**
SCIENTIFIC NAME:	*Xiphophorus maculatus.*
SYNONYMS:	*Platypoecilus maculatus, Poecilia maculata.*
SIZE:	Males up to 3.5 cm (1.5 in); females 6 cm (2.5 in).
RANGE:	Mexico (Vera Cruz) to Belize.
NATURAL HABITAT:	Quiet stretches of water.
WATER CONDITIONS:	Neutral to slightly alkaline conditions preferred but will tolerate a range. Temperature around 24°c (75°F).
DIET:	Will accept most foods which should include a vegetable component.
NOTES:	Hybridises easily with Swordtails and Sunset Platies. Numerous varieties are available.

COMMON NAMES:	**Sunset or Variatus Platy.**
SCIENTIFIC NAME:	*Xiphophorus variatus.*
SYNONYMS:	*Platypoecilus variatus, Platypoecilus maculatus.*
SIZE:	Males up to 5.5 cm (2.2 in); females 7 cm (2.75 in).
RANGE:	Mexico (Atlantic Slope).
NATURAL HABITAT:	Quiet stretches of water.
WATER CONDITIONS, DIET, AND NOTES:	As for *X. maculatus.*

COMMON NAMES:	**Sphenops, Black Molly, Green Molly, Liberty Molly.**
SCIENTIFIC NAME:	*Poecilia sphenops.*
SYNONYMS:	*Mollienisia sphenops, Mollienisia gracilis.*
SIZE:	Up to 10 cm (4 in).
RANGE:	From northeast Mexico southwards into northern South America.
NATURAL HABITAT:	Fresh or brackish waters.
WATER CONDITIONS:	Slightly hard and alkaline with a teaspoonful of salt per gallon. Temperature 25–28°c (77–82°F).
DIET:	Will accept most foods but diet must include a vegetable component.
NOTES:	Not a very easy species for beginners. Many varieties are available.

Platy

Sunset or **Variatus Platy**

Sphenops, Liberty Molly

COMMON NAMES:	**Sailfin Molly** or **Yucatán Sailfin**
SCIENTIFIC NAMES:	(i) *Poecilia latipinna*; (ii) *P. velifera.*
SYNONYMS:	(i) *Mollienisia latipinna*; (ii) *M. velifera.*
SIZE:	(i) *P. latipinna* – males up to 10 cm (4 in); females 12 cm (4.7 in) (ii) *P. velifera* – males up to 15 cm (6 in); females 18 cm (7 in), but usually a lot smaller.
RANGE:	(i) *P. latipinna* – southeastern USA, southwards into Mexico. (ii) *P. velifera* – Mexico (Yucatán – hence its alternative name, the Yucatán Sailfin).
NATURAL HABITAT:	Coastal fresh, brackish and salt water.
WATER CONDITIONS:	As for *P. sphenops* – higher end of the temperature range preferred.
DIET:	As for *P. sphenops.*
NOTES:	These species are very similar to each other and will interbreed easily with *P. sphenops*. Many varieties are available. Neither species can be regarded as easy for beginners.

COMMON NAMES:	**Cuban Limia, Banded Limia.**
SCIENTIFIC NAME:	*Poecilia vittata.*
SYNONYM:	*Limia vittata.*
SIZE:	Males up to about 6.5 cm (2.5 in); females 10 cm (4 in).
RANGE:	Cuba.
NATURAL HABITAT:	Slow moving or still waters, often with abundant vegetation.
WATER CONDITIONS:	Neutral or slightly alkaline. Temperature around 25°C (77°F).
DIET:	Will accept a wide range of foods which should include a vegetable component.
NOTES:	This is a peaceful, attractive species which will hybridise with other Limias, such as the Blue Limia (*Poecilia melanogaster*) and the Humpbacked Limia (*Poecilia nigrofasciata*).

COMMON NAME:	**Mosquito Fish** (see Notes).
SCIENTIFIC NAMES:	(i) *Gambusia affinis affinis*; (ii) *G. affinis holbrooki.*
SYNONYM:	None.
SIZE:	Males around 3 cm (1.2 in); females 6.5 cm (2.5 in).
RANGE:	(i) Originally largely confined to Texas; (ii) southeastern USA.
NATURAL HABITAT:	Wide range of still and moving bodies of fresh and brackish water.
WATER CONDITIONS:	Extreme range of conditions tolerated. Temperature: (reportedly) from near-freezing to above 30°C (86°F).
DIET:	Will eat virtually any food offered.
NOTES:	Both subspecies have been widely introduced in tropical and subtropical areas for biological control of malarial mosquitoes. *G. affinis holbrooki* sometimes occurs as a melanic (black) form. Gambusias are quite aggressive and cannibalistic towards their own young.

Sailfin Molly

Cuban Limia, male (lower); **Blue Limia**, female (upper)

Mosquito Fish

Some Other Poeciliids Occasionally Available

Common Name	Scientific Name	Size cm (in) Male	Female	Habits	Water Conditions	Diet
Merry Widow	*Phallichthys amates amates*	4 (1.6)	4.5 (1.8)	Peaceful	Slightly alkaline. Around 24°c (75°F)	Most foods. Some vegetable matter
Bishop	*Brachyraphis episcopi*	3.5 (1.4)	5 (2)	Lively. Often nips fins	Not critical. Around 24°c (75°F)	Most foods
Girardinus	*Girardinus metallicus*	4.5 (1.8)	6.5 (2.6)	Lively but not aggressive	Clean water. Around 24°c (75°F)	Most foods. Some vegetable matter
Pike Livebearer	*Belonesox belizanus*	9 (3.5)	10 (3.9)	Predatory	Not critical but should have one teaspoonful of salt per gallon. Around 24°c (75°F)	Livefoods
Knife Livebearer	*Alfaro cultratus*	5 (2)	7 (2.75)	Lively but not aggressive	Clean water. Around 25°c (77°F)	Most foods. Should include livefoods.
Swordtail Platy	*Xiphophorus xiphidium*	3 (1.2)	4 (1.6)	Peaceful and delicate	Clean, slightly alkaline water. Around 25°c (77°F)	Most foods. Some vegetable matter
Liberty Molly	*Poecilia sphenops*	8 (3.15)	10 (3.9)		See Black/Green Molly	

Family Anablepidae (Subfamily Anablepinae)

COMMON NAME: **Four-eyed Fish.**

SCIENTIFIC NAME: *Anableps anableps.*

SYNONYM: None.

SIZE: Around 30 cm (12 in).

RANGE: Northern South America and southern Mexico.

NATURAL HABITAT: Brackish (usually slow-moving) streams and canals.

WATER CONDITIONS: Hard, alkaline water with one teaspoonful of salt per gallon is preferred. Temperature around 27°c (*c* 80.5°F).

DIET: Livefoods but will also eat frozen foods, meat and fish.

NOTES: Not an easy species. Unusual eye structure allows for simultaneous aerial and underwater vision. Some males can only swing their gonopodium to either the right or the left. Females may also be 'right- or left-handed'.

Four-eyed Fish

One-sided Livebearer

Family Jenynsiidae (Subfamily Anablepinae)

COMMON NAME:	**One-sided Livebearer.**
SCIENTIFIC NAME:	*Jenynsia lineata.*
SYNONYMS:	*J. pygogramma, J. maculata.*
SIZE:	Males around 4 cm (1.5 in); females 6 cm (2.5 in).
RANGE:	Southern South America.
NATURAL HABITAT:	Still or slow-moving waters.
WATER CONDITIONS:	Raw water should be avoided, mature water is preferred. Temperature 24°C (75°F).
DIET:	Will eat many foods but should receive a regular supply of livefoods.
NOTES:	Males may be dextral ('right-handed') or sinistral ('left-handed') as in *Anableps*. Similarly for females.

Family Goodeidae (Subfamily Goodeinae)

COMMON NAMES:	**Ameca, Butterfly Goodeid.**
SCIENTIFIC NAME:	*Ameca splendens.*
SYNONYM:	None.
SIZE:	Males around 7.5 cm (3 in); females 9 cm (3.5 in).
RANGE:	Río Ameca Basin, Mexico.
NATURAL HABITAT:	Moving water.
WATER CONDITIONS:	Not critical but slightly alkaline water with a small amount of salt seems to be preferred. Temperature 22–29°c (71–84°F).
DIET:	Will eat most foods but these should include a vegetable component.
NOTES:	Some specimens may become fin-nippers. Fry are very large, having received nourishment from the mother via structures known as Trophotaeniae.

COMMON NAMES:	**Orange or Red-tailed Goodeid.**
SCIENTIFIC NAME:	*Xenotoca eiseni.*
SYNONYM:	*Characodon eiseni.*
SIZE:	Males around 7.5 cm (3 in); females 10 cm (4 in).
RANGE:	Northwest and southeast Mexico.
NATURAL HABITAT:	Often shallow waters with abundant vegetation.
WATER CONDITIONS:	Not critical but alkaline, medium hard water seems best. Temperature 20–29°c (70–84°F).
DIET:	Will eat most things but requires a vegetable component.
NOTES:	As for *Ameca splendens.*

Family Exocoetidae

COMMON NAMES:	**Malayan** or **Wrestling Half Beak.**
SCIENTIFIC NAME:	*Dermogenys pusillus.*
SYNONYM:	None.
SIZE:	Males about 6 cm (2.5 in); females 8 cm (3.2 in).
RANGE:	Far East.
NATURAL HABITAT:	A variety of fresh and brackish waters.
WATER CONDITIONS:	Not critical but may include a teaspoonful of salt per gallon. Temperature 20–30°c (68–86°F).
DIET:	Predominance of livefoods must be supplied.
NOTES:	A predatory, difficult species. Males aggressive towards each other.

Ameca, Butterfly Goodeid

Orange or **Red-tailed Goodeid**

Malayan or **Wrestling Half Beak**

Egglayers

These fish are represented in tropical aquaria by species from numerous families. Among these are the Characins (Characidae), Cichlids (Cichlidae), Catfishes (Callichthyidae, Loricariidae, Mochokidae, and others), Anabantoids (Anabantidae, Belontiidae and others), Cyprinids (Cyprinidae, the largest family with about 1600 species, among them the Carps, Rasboras, Barbs, Danios and some 'Sharks'), Killifishes (Cyprinodontidae – according to traditional classifications), Spiny Eels (Mastacembelidae) and numerous others.

Egglayers, despite marked differences in shape, size, colour and behaviour, share several characteristics. The most obvious of these is the external fertilisation of eggs. There are exceptions to this – such as *Cynolebias brucei*, a Killifish which employs internal fertilisation and then lays eggs – but they are few.

Family Characidae

COMMON NAMES:	(i) **Neon Tetra;**
	(ii) **Cardinal Tetra.**
SCIENTIFIC NAMES:	(i) *Paracheirodon innesi*;
	(ii) *Paracheirodon axelrodi.*
SYNONYMS:	(i) *Hyphessobrycon innesi*;
	(ii) *Cheirodon axelrodi, Hyphessobrycon cardinalis.*
SIZE:	Neon up to 4 cm (1.5 in); Cardinal 5 cm (2 in) but usually smaller.
RANGE:	South America:
	(i) upper Amazon (Neon);
	(ii) upper Río Negro (Cardinal).
NATURAL HABITAT:	Small jungle pools and streams.
WATER CONDITIONS:	Soft acid water. Temperature 22–25°c 71.5–77°f).
DIET:	Most foods.
NOTES:	Both species are egg-scatterers and should be kept in shoals. Cardinals are more colourful with the red pigmentation stretching the length of the body.

COMMON NAMES:	**Blind Cave Fish, Characin, Tetra.**
SCIENTIFIC NAME:	*Astyanax fasciatus mexicanus.*
SYNONYMS:	*Anoptichthys jordani, Astyanax jordani.*
SIZE:	About 9 cm (3.5 in).
RANGE:	Caves around San Luis Potosí, Mexico.
NATURAL HABITAT:	Underground streams and lakes.
WATER CONDITIONS:	Slightly hard and alkaline. Temperature 20–30°c (68–86°f).
DIET:	Most foods.
NOTES:	There is still some ambiguity concerning the exact status of this fish, but agreement is widespread that *Anoptichthys* is not a valid generic name and that this fish is a blind cave morph of normally sighted and pigmented ancestors.

Neon Tetra

Cardinal Tetra

Blind Cave Fish

Some Other Tetras Commonly Available

Common Name	Scientific Name	Size cm (in)	Habits	Water Conditions	Diet
Splashing Tetra	*Copella (Copeina) arnoldi	7 (2.75)	Peaceful	Neutral to slightly acid. 24–26°c (75–79°F)	Most foods but livefoods preferred
Black Widow	Gymno-corymbus ternetzi	5 (2)	Peaceful	Not critical: 24–28°c (75–82°F)	Most foods but surface insects preferred
Silver Tip or Copper Tetra	Hasemania marginata	4 (1.6)	Peaceful	Not critical. 22–25°c (71.5–77°F)	As for Black Widow
Buenos Aires Tetra	Hemigrammus caudovittatus	7 (2.75)	Lively but generally peaceful	Not critical. 22–26°c (71.5–79°F)	Most foods which should include a vegetable component
Glowlight Tetra	Hemigrammus erythrozonus	4.5 (1.8)	Peaceful	As for Silver Tip	As for Black Widow
Head-and-tail Light Tetra (Beacon Fish)	Hemigrammus ocellifer	4 (1.6)	Peaceful	As for Silver Tip	Most foods – diet should include livefoods. Tubifex accepted reluctantly
Rummy-nosed Tetra	Hemigrammus rhodostomus	4 (1.6)	Peaceful	Not critical. 23–25°c (73.5–77°F)	As for Head-and-tail Light Tetra
Bleeding Heart Tetra	Hyphessobrycon erythrostigma	8 (3.15)	Generally peaceful	Not critical but softish, slightly acid water is preferred. 23–27°c (73.5–80.5°F)	Most foods with regular supplies of surface livefoods
Flame Tetra	Hyphessobrycon flammeus	4.5 (1.8)	Peaceful	Soft, slightly acid water preferred. 22–26°c (71.5–79°F)	As for Bleeding Heart Tetra
Black Neon	Hyphessobrycon herbert-axelrodi	4 (1.6)	Lively but peaceful	Soft, neutral to slightly acid water preferred. 21–26°c (70–79°F)	Most foods – diet should include livefoods
Flag Tetra	Hyphessobrycon heterorhabdus	5 (2)	Shy	Soft, slightly acid water. 24°c (75°F)	Livefoods preferred
Lemon Tetra	Hyphessobrycon pulchripinnis	5 (2)	Peaceful	As for Flag Tetra. 22–26°c (71.5–79°F)	As for Bleeding Heart Tetra
Serpae Tetra	Hyphessobrycon serpae	4.5 (1.8)	Peaceful	As for Flame Tetra	As for Bleeding Heart Tetra
Emperor Tetra	Nematobrycon palmeri	6 (2.4)	Males may be aggressive towards each other	Not critical but softish, old aquarium water preferred. 24°c (75°F)	Most foods
Congo Tetra	Phenaco-grammus interruptus	8 (3.15)	Peaceful	Slightly acid water that is not too hard preferred. 24°c (75°F)	Livefoods preferred but will take other types
Penguin Fish	Thayeria obliqua	7 (2.75)	Peaceful	Soft, slightly acid water preferred. 23–28°c (73.5–82°F)	As for Congo Tetra

All the listed species are shoalers to a greater or lesser extent and scatter their eggs. A notable exception is *Copella (Copeina) arnoldi* which sticks its eggs on a leaf above the water surface and guards them until they hatch, keeping them moist by splashing water onto them.

* Copella is included in this Table because it is commonly known as a Tetra. However, it is classified in the family Lebiasinidae (along with the Pencilfishes) by Greenwood and others.

Red or **Natterer's Piranha**

Silver Dollar, Metynnis

COMMON NAMES:	**Red or Natterer's Piranha.**
SCIENTIFIC NAME:	*Serrasalmus nattereri.*
SYNONYM:	*Rooseveltiella nattereri.*
SIZE:	Up to 30 cm (12 in)
RANGE:	Amazon and Orinoco basins.
NATURAL HABITAT:	Open waters.
WATER CONDITIONS:	Soft, slightly acid water. Temperature 24–27° c (75–80° F).
DIET:	Raw fish and meat.
NOTES:	Most Piranha species are shoaling predators in the wild. In captivity, shoals are only feasible in very large aquaria. Handle with care! All Piranha are egg-scatterers.

COMMON NAMES:	**Silver Dollar, Schreitmueller's Metynnis.**
SCIENTIFIC NAME:	*Metynnis hypsauchen* (see Notes)
SYNONYM:	*Metynnis schreitmuelleri.*
SIZE:	Up to 15 cm (6 in).
RANGE:	Amazon.
NATURAL HABITAT:	Slow-moving vegetated waters.
WATER CONDITIONS:	Not critical, but preferably slightly acid. Temperature 24–27° c (75–80° F).
DIET:	Live or frozen foods with a generous vegetable component.
NOTES:	There is no universal agreement concerning the synonym of this peaceful, shoaling, egg-scattering species.

Family Anostomidae

COMMON NAMES:	**Striped Anostomus, Striped Headstander.**
SCIENTIFIC NAME:	*Anostomus anostomus.*
SYNONYM:	None.
SIZE:	14 cm (5.5 in).
RANGE:	Upper reaches of the Amazon, western Guyana.
NATURAL HABITAT:	Still or slow-moving waters with densely vegetated banks.
WATER CONDITIONS:	Not critical but peaty water seems to be preferred. Temperature 25–27° c (77–80.5° f).
DIET:	Most foods; diet should include vegetable matter.
NOTES:	The common name Headstander is derived from the unusual angle adopted by these fish while at rest. No detailed reports of captive breeding are available. *A. anostomus* can be a bit intolerant of other species at times.

Family Distichodontidae
(see *Notes*)

COMMON NAME:	**Long-nosed Distichodus.**
SCIENTIFIC NAME:	*Distichodus lusosso.*
SYNONYM:	None.
SIZE:	Around 30 cm (12 in)
RANGE:	Angola, middle and upper Zaire.
NATURAL HABITAT:	Variety of waters.
WATER CONDITIONS:	Neutral or slightly acid. Temperature 24–27° c (75–80.5° f).
DIET:	Livefoods preferred; diet should also include vegetable matter.
NOTES:	*Distichodus lusosso* is a peaceful fish despite its size – it has not yet been bred in aquaria.

Family Hemiodontidae
(see *Notes* and *Lebiasinidae*)

COMMON NAMES:	**Half-lined** or **Silver Hemiodus.**
SCIENTIFIC NAME:	*Hemiodopsis semitaeniatus.*
SYNONYM:	*Hemiodus semitaeniatus.*
SIZE:	20 cm (8 in).
RANGE:	Guyanas, middle and lower Amazon, Mato Grosso (Brazil).
NATURAL HABITAT:	Variety of waters.
WATER CONDITIONS:	Not critical. Temperature 23–28° c (73.5–82° f).
DIET:	Livefoods preferred but other foods also taken.
NOTES:	*H. semitaeniatus* is an active shoaling species which does not appear to have been bred successfully in aquaria. It is usually tolerant of other species.

Striped Anostomus, Striped Headstander

Long-nosed Distichodus

Half-lined or **Silver Hemiodus**

Family Lebiasinidae
(see *Notes* and *Hemiodontidae*)

COMMON NAME:	**Golden Pencilfish.**
SCIENTIFIC NAME:	*Nannostomus beckfordi.*
SYNONYM:	*Nannobrycon beckfordi.*
SIZE:	5 cm (2 in).
RANGE:	South America.
NATURAL HABITAT:	Slow-moving waters with heavily vegetated, shady banks.
WATER CONDITIONS:	Soft, acid water is preferred. Temperature 24–28°C (75–82°F).
DIET:	Small livefoods are preferred.
NOTES:	Pencilfishes have traditonally been classified in the family Hemiodontidae or (earlier) in the Nannostomidae. However, many leading authorities regard them as belonging to the Lebiasinidae. Some species show very marked differences between day and night coloration. Males will often become aggressive towards each other. Eggs are laid on fine-leaved vegetation. No parental care occurs.

Family Cyprinidae

COMMON NAMES:	**Tiger** or **Sumatra Barb.**
SCIENTIFIC NAME:	*Barbus tetrazona.*
SYNONYMS:	*Capoeta tetrazona, Puntius tetrazona, Barbodes tetrazona* and others.
SIZE:	Up to 7 cm (2.75 in), usually less.
RANGE:	Borneo, Indonesia (particularly Sumatra).
NATURAL HABITAT:	Wide variety of still and flowing waters.
WATER CONDITIONS:	Not critical, but soft, slightly acid water preferred for spawning. Temperature 20–29°C (68–84°F).
DIET:	Most foods.
NOTES:	There are several artificial varieties, e.g. Albino and Green. In addition, numerous similar species or subspecies exist. *B. tetrazona* is a lively egg-scattering shoaler which tends to nip fins when kept singly or in pairs.

COMMON NAMES:	**Tinfoil, Goldfoil** or **Schwanenfeld's Barb.**
SCIENTIFIC NAME:	*Barbus schwanenfeldi.*
SYNONYM:	*Barbodes schwanenfeldi.*
SIZE:	Up to 35 cm (13.8 in), usually less.
RANGE:	Borneo, Indonesia (particularly Sumatra), Moluccas, Thailand.
NATURAL HABITAT:	Well-oxygenated waters.
WATER CONDITIONS:	Soft, slightly acid water is preferred. Raw water must be avoided. Temperature 22–25°C (71.5–77°F).
DIET:	All foods – vegetable component must be included.
NOTE:	This is a large, lively, egg-scattering shoaler with excellent jumping ability.

Golden Pencilfish

Tiger or **Sumatra Barb**

Tinfoil, Goldfoil or **Schwanenfeld's Barb**

COMMON NAME:	**Cherry Barb.**
SCIENTIFIC NAME:	*Barbus titteya.*
SYNONYM:	*Copoeta titteya.*
SIZE:	Around 5 cm (2 in)
RANGE:	Sri Lanka.
NATURAL HABITAT:	Shaded or overgrown streams.
WATER CONDITIONS:	Soft and slightly acid. Temperature 22–24°c (71.5–75°f).
DIET:	Most foods – should receive some vegetable matter.
NOTES:	Some specimens can be shy and retiring. Dense clumps of vegetation should, therefore, be provided. Shoaling instinct exists but it is not acutely developed in this egg-scattering species.

COMMON NAME:	**Rosy Barb.**
SCIENTIFIC NAME:	*Barbus conchonius.*
SYNONYM:	*Puntius conchonius.*
SIZE:	Around 10 cm (4 in).
RANGE:	Assam, Bengal, Northern India.
NATURAL HABITAT:	Still and flowing waters.
WATER CONDITIONS:	Not critical but raw water should be avoided. Temperature around 15°c (59°f) in winter, 22–25°c (71.5–77°f) in summer.
DIET:	All foods – should receive livefoods on a regular basis.
NOTES:	There is also a long-finned aquarium variety of this egg-scattering species.

COMMON NAMES:	**Ruby, Black Ruby** or **Purple-headed Barb.**
SCIENTIFIC NAME:	*Barbus nigrofasciatus.*
SYNONYM:	*Puntius nigrofasciatus.*
SIZE:	Around 6 cm (2.5 in)
RANGE:	Sri Lanka.
NATURAL HABITAT:	Slow-flowing waters.
WATER CONDITIONS:	Not critical but raw water must be avoided. Temperature 23–25°c (73.5–77°f).
DIET:	All foods, which should include a regular supply of live material.
NOTES:	A shoaling, egg-scattering species which suffers badly in raw water.

Cherry Barb

Rosy Barb

Ruby, Black Ruby or **Purple-headed Barb**

COMMON NAME:	**Golden Barb.**
SCIENTIFIC NAME:	*Barbus schuberti* (see Notes).
SYNONYM:	None.
SIZE:	Around 7 cm (2.75 in)
RANGE:	See Notes.
NATURAL HABITAT:	See Notes.
WATER CONDITIONS:	Not critical but raw water should be avoided. Temperature 20–24° c (68–75° F).
DIET:	All foods.
NOTES:	This species appears to be man-made, probably developed from *Barbus semifasciolatus*, the Green Barb with which it interbreeds freely. If so, then *B. schuberti* is not a valid species at all. It is a prolific egg-scatterer.

COMMON NAME:	**Odessa Barb.**
SCIENTIFIC NAME:	None (see Notes).
SYNONYM:	None.
SIZE:	Around 6 cm (2.5 in).
RANGE:	See Notes.
NATURAL HABITAT:	See Notes.
WATER CONDITIONS:	Not critical. Temperature 21–30° c (70–86° F).
DIET:	All foods.
NOTES:	Opinions vary as to the origin of this fish. It is believed by some to be a variety of *Barbus ticto* (from Sri Lanka). Others believe it to be a man-made fish arising from crosses involving various of the following: *B. conchonius* (Rosy Barb), *B. cumingi* (Cuming's Barb), *B. ticto* (Ticto Barb) or *B. ticto stoliczkae* (Stoliczk's Barb – also known as *B. stoliczkanus*). The Odessa Barb is a prolific egg-scatterer.

Golden Barb

Some Other Barbs Available

Common Name	Scientific Name	Size cm (in)	Habits	Water Conditions	Diet
Long-finned or Arulius Barb	*Barbus arulius (Capoeta arulia)*	12 (4.7)	Lively	Not critical. 23–25°C (73.5–77°F)	All foods
African Two-spot Barb	*Barbus bimaculatus (Capoeta puckelli)*	6 (2.4)	Peaceful	Soft, slightly acid water preferred. 24–26°C (75–79°F)	All foods
Striped or Zebra Barb	*Barbus (Barbodes) fasciatus*	12 (4.7)	Quite lively	Soft, slightly acid water. 22–25°C (71.5–77°F)	All foods
African Banded Barb	*Barbus (Barbodes) fasciolatus*	7 (2.75)	Males may be aggressive	Not critical. 22–25°C (71.5–77°F)	All foods
Black-spot Barb	*Barbus (Puntius) filamentosus*	12.5 (4.9)	Peaceful with similarly sized fish	Not critical but slightly acid water preferred. 24–26°C (75–79°F)	All foods
Dwarf Barb	*Barbus (Puntius) gelius*	4 (1.6)	Peaceful	Not critical. 18–22°C (64.5–71.5°F)	All foods
Spanner Barb	*Barbus (Barbodes) lateristriga*	13 (5.1)	Lively; peaceful when small	Not critical but soft, old water preferred. 25°C (77°F)	All foods
Checker or Island Barb	*Barbus (Capoeta) oligolepis*	5 (2)	Lively but peaceful	Not critical but soft, slightly acid water preferred. 24–26°C (75–79°F)	All foods
Ocellated Barb	*Barbus rhomboocellatus (Barbodes pentazona rhomboocellatus)*	6 (2.4)	Lively and generally peaceful	Not critical. 24–30°C (75–86°F)	All foods
Livebearing or Silver barb (*NB* It is an egglayer like all Barbs).	*Barbus viviparus*	6.5 (2.6)	Large specimens may eat small fry. Otherwise peaceful	Not critical. 25°C (77°F)	All foods

Odessa Barb

COMMON NAME:	**Red-tailed Black Shark.**
SCIENTIFIC NAME:	*Labeo bicolor.*
SYNONYM:	None.
SIZE:	Up to 15 cm (6 in).
RANGE:	Thailand.
NATURAL HABITAT:	Mainly in flowing streams.
WATER CONDITIONS:	Mature, neutral to slightly alkaline, soft to medium hard water preferred. Temperature 24–27°c (75–80°f).
DIET:	Many foods, particularly bottom-dwelling livefoods. A vegetable component must be included.
NOTES:	Some specimens can be somewhat aggressive. Other sharks include the similar, but slimmer Red-finned Shark (*L. erythrurus*) – also found in the albino form. No detailed accounts of natural spawnings are available.

COMMON NAMES:	**Bala, Malayan, Silver** or **Tricolour Shark.**
SCIENTIFIC NAME:	*Balantiocheilus melanopterus.*
SYNONYM:	None.
SIZE:	35 cm (13.8 in), usually smaller.
RANGE:	Thailand.
NATURAL HABITAT:	Flowing waters.
WATER CONDITIONS:	Not critical but neutral to slightly alkaline water preferred. Temperature 23–26°c (73.5–79°f).
DIET:	All foods. Some individuals may prove a bit difficult and will only feed on livefoods.
NOTES:	This is a very active but quite peaceful species. It is an excellent jumper. No reports of captive spawning are available.

COMMON NAME:	**Flying Fox.**
SCIENTIFIC NAME:	*Epalzeorhynchus kallopterus.*
SYNONYM:	None.
SIZE:	14 cm (5.5 in), usually smaller.
RANGE:	Borneo and Indonesia (particularly Java and Sumatra).
NATURAL HABITAT:	Shallow waters with vegetated banks.
WATER CONDITIONS:	Soft, slightly acid water preferred. Temperature 23–26°c (73.5–79°f).
DIET:	Will accept most foods. Should receive vegetable matter on a regular basis.
NOTES:	This is a fast-swimming fish which is tolerant of other species but often intolerant of its own kind. No reports of successful spawnings in aquaria are available.

Red-tailed Shark

Bala, Malayan, Silver or **Tricolour Shark**

Flying Fox

COMMON NAMES:	**Harlequin, Red Rasbora.**
SCIENTIFIC NAME:	*Rasbora heteromorpha.*
SYNONYM:	None.
SIZE:	Up to 4.5 cm (1.8 in).
RANGE:	Malay Peninsula, Sumatra, Thailand.
NATURAL HABITAT:	Marshy pools, shady and mountain streams.
WATER CONDITIONS:	Matured, soft, slightly acid water. Temperature 24–27°c (75–80°f).
DIET:	Most foods. Bottom livefoods, such as *Tubifex*, should be avoided.
NOTES:	A similar but less colourful and slimmer species, *R. hengeli*, can easily be confused with the Harlequin. Eggs are laid on the underside of a leaf.

COMMON NAMES:	**Two-spot, Big-spot** or **Clown Rasbora.**
SCIENTIFIC NAME:	*Rasbora kalochroma.*
SYNONYM:	None.
SIZE:	Around 10 cm (4 in).
RANGE:	Borneo, Malaya and Sumatra.
NATURAL HABITAT:	Still and slow-flowing waters.
WATER CONDITIONS:	Soft, slightly acid, mature water. Temperature 25–28°c (77–82°f).
DIET:	Most foods, including small surface insects, e.g. mosquito larvae.
NOTES:	This is an active but peaceful shoaler. No detailed reports of spawning in aquaria are yet available.

COMMON NAMES:	**Three-line Rasbora, Scissortail.**
SCIENTIFIC NAME:	*Rasbora trilineata.*
SYNONYM:	None.
SIZE:	Around 12 cm (4.8 in).
RANGE:	Malaysia.
NATURAL HABITAT:	Still and slow-flowing waters.
WATER CONDITIONS:	Not critical but soft, acid water preferred. Temperature 22–25°c (71.5–77°f).
DIET:	Most foods. Surface livefoods greedily accepted.
NOTES:	This lively but peaceful species looks best in a shoal. It is an egg scatterer.

Harlequin, Red Rasbora

Two-spot, Big-spot or **Clown Rasbora**

Three-line Rasbora, Scissortail

COMMON NAMES:	**Red-line, Red Striped** or **Glowlight Rasbora.**
SCIENTIFIC NAME:	*Rasbora pauciperforata.*
SYNONYM:	None.
SIZE:	Up to 6 cm (2.5 in).
RANGE:	Indonesia.
NATURAL HABITAT:	Streams and other small water channels.
WATER CONDITIONS:	Not critical but soft, acid water preferred. Temperature 19–21°c (66–70°F) in winter; 23–26°c (73.5–79°F) in summer.
DIET:	Livefoods are preferred.
NOTES:	This is a shy egg-scattering species; likes having shady areas in which to shelter. *R. pauciperforata* has been spawned only occasionally in aquaria.

COMMON NAMES:	**Dwarf, Pigmy** or **Spotted Rasbora.**
SCIENTIFIC NAME:	*Rasbora maculata.*
SYNONYM:	None.
SIZE:	About 2.5 cm (1 in).
RANGE:	Indonesia, Malaysia.
NATURAL HABITAT:	Still and slow-moving densely vegetated waters.
WATER CONDITIONS:	Soft, slightly acid, mature water preferred. Temperature 22–26°c (71.5–79°F).
DIET:	Small livefoods, but commercial foods also accepted.
NOTES:	This is the smallest of the *Rasbora* species. It is a shy, egg-scattering peaceful fish which should not be kept with larger, more active species.

COMMON NAME:	**Zebra Danio.**
SCIENTIFIC NAME:	*Brachydanio rerio.*
SYNONYM:	None.
SIZE:	Around 4.5 cm (1.8 in).
RANGE:	Eastern India.
NATURAL HABITAT:	Still and slow-flowing waters.
WATER CONDITIONS:	Not critical but raw water should be avoided. Temperature 20–24°c (68–75°F).
DIET:	Most foods.
NOTES:	This is a lively but tolerant shoaling species which scatters its eggs. There is a long-finned man-made variety which is not as robust as the wild type.

Red-line, Red Striped or **Glowlight Rasbora**

Dwarf, Pigmy or **Spotted Rasbora**

Zebra Danio

COMMON NAME:	**Leopard Danio.**
SCIENTIFIC NAME:	*Brachydanio frankei.*
SYNONYM:	None.
SIZE:	Around 5.5 cm (2.2 in).
RANGE:	See Notes.
NATURAL HABITAT:	See Notes.
WATER CONDITIONS:	Not critical but raw water should be avoided. Temperature 20–24° c (68–75° F).
DIET:	Most foods.
NOTES:	This 'species' is not known with any certainty from the wild. It has been suggested that it occurs in Thailand but other opinions point towards it being a mutant strain of *B. rerio* or *B. nigrofasciatus*. If this proves to be the case, the name *B. frankei* would become invalid for this peaceful, shoaling egg-scatterer.

Long-finned Leopard Danio

Other Danios Available

Common Name	Scientific Name	Size cm (in)	Habits	Water conditions	Diet
Pearl Danio	*Brachydanio alboli-neatus*	5.5 (2.2)	Lively, peaceful shoaler	Not critical. 22–24° c (71.5–75° F)	Most foods
Blue or Kerr's Danio	*Brachydanio kerri*	5.5 (2.2)	As above	Not critical. 20–24° c (68–75° F)	As above
Dwarf or Spotted Danio	*Brachydanio nigrofasciatus*	4.5 (1.8)	As above	Not critical. 22–25° c (71.5–77° F)	As above
Bengal Danio	*Danio devario*	8 (3.2)	As above	Not critical. 24° c (75° F)	As above
Giant Danio	*Danio malabaricus (aequipinnatus)*	10 (3.9)	As above	As above	As above

Family Cichlidae

COMMON NAMES:	**Angelfish, Scalare.**
SCIENTIFIC NAME:	*Pterophyllum scalare.*
SYNONYM:	*Pterophyllum eimekei.*
SIZE:	Around 12 cm (4.7 in).
RANGE:	Amazon basin.
NATURAL HABITAT:	Still and slow-moving waters, often heavily overgrown.
WATER CONDITIONS:	Not critical but soft, slightly acid water preferred. Temperature 23–27° C (73–80° F).
DIET:	All foods, particularly swimming livefoods.
NOTES:	There are numerous varieties of Angelfish all of which interbreed easily. Eggs are laid on a pre-cleaned leaf or other semivertical surface and guarded by the spawning pair.

Angelfish, Scalare

COMMON NAMES:	**Discus, Pompadour Fish.**
SCIENTIFIC NAMES:	*Symphysodon discus, S. aequifasciata* (see Notes).
SYNONYMS:	See Notes.
SIZE:	Up to 15 cm (6 in).
RANGE:	Amazon Basin.
NATURAL HABITAT:	Still waters with a degree of overgrowth.
WATER CONDITIONS:	Soft, slightly acid water is a must for prolonged maintenance. Temperature 25–30°C (77–86°F) or even slightly higher.
DIET:	Small livefoods preferred. Minced ox-heart and some commercial foods also accepted.
NOTES:	There are only two nominal species of Discus (see above). However, they are very similar to each other and hybridise easily. In addition, natural varieties and subspecies and man-made forms make identification very difficult. They include: *S. discus, S. aequifasciata aequifasciata, S. a. axelrodi and S. a. haraldi.* Eggs are usually laid on a flat surface. Parents secrete a nourishing body mucus from which the fry feed. Discus can be difficult to maintain in peak condition.

COMMON NAMES:	**Oscar, Peacock-eye Cichlid, Velvet Cichlid.**
SCIENTIFIC NAME:	*Astronotus ocellatus.*
SYNONYM:	None.
SIZE:	Up to 30 cm (12 in).
RANGE:	Northern South America.
NATURAL HABITAT:	Wide variety of waters.
WATER CONDITIONS:	Not critical. Temperature 20–25°C (68–77°F).
DIET:	All large foods. Meat/fish component required.
NOTES:	Usually sold as small, attractively marked specimens. Several varieties available. Eggs laid on pre-cleaned surface. Eggs and fry are guarded by both parents. Adults sometimes become quite tame but may be aggressive towards other fish.

COMMON NAME:	**Firemouth.**
SCIENTIFIC NAME:	*Cichlasoma (Thorichthys) meeki.*
SYNONYM:	*Cichlasoma hyorhynchum.*
SIZE:	Males up to 15 cm (6 in); females 11.5 cm (4.5 in).
RANGE:	Mexico (including Yucatán), Northern Guatemala.
NATURAL HABITAT:	Still and slow-flowing waters, including sink-holes (Cenotes) in Northern Yucatán.
WATER CONDITIONS:	Alkaline, hard water. Temperature 24–28°C (75–82°F).
DIET:	All foods.
NOTES:	Eggs are usually laid on a vertical surface under cover. Eggs and fry are vigorously protected by both parents. Some plants may be dug up during spawning period. Males may be aggressive towards each other.

Discus, Pompadour Fish

Oscar, Peacock-eye Cichlid, Velvet Cichlid

Firemouth

COMMON NAME:	**Festive Cichlid.**
SCIENTIFIC NAME:	*Mesonauta festivus.*
SYNONYM:	*Cichlasoma festivum.*
SIZE:	Up to 15 cm (6 in), usually smaller.
RANGE:	Amazon Basin.
NATURAL HABITAT:	Still and slow-moving waters.
WATER CONDITIONS:	Fairly soft, slightly acid water. Temperature 22–26°c (71.5–79°F).
DIET:	Most foods, should include a vegetable supplement.
NOTES:	This is a peaceful Cichlid except during spawning. Eggs are laid on a flat stone or sturdy leaves. Parents are protective of eggs and young.

COMMON NAMES:	**Congo, Convict** or **Zebra Cichlid.**
SCIENTIFIC NAME:	*Cichlasoma (Archocentrus) nigrofasciatum* (see Notes).
SYNONYM:	*Heros nigrofasciatus.*
SIZE:	10 cm (4 in).
RANGE:	Central America, Guatemala.
NATURAL HABITAT:	Lakes, streams and rivers.
WATER CONDITIONS:	Not critical. Temperature 22–25°c (71.5–77°F) but will tolerate considerably lower temperatures.
DIET:	All foods, including animal and vegetable matter.
NOTES:	The generic name *Archocentrus* has been proposed but has not yet received universal acceptance. This is a pugnacious species which lays its eggs on a prepared site and guards its offspring vigorously. There is also a golden aquarium form which does not occur in the wild.

COMMON NAMES:	**Banded Cichlid, Severum.**
SCIENTIFIC NAME:	*Cichlasoma (Heros) severum.*
SYNONYM:	See Notes.
SIZE:	20 cm (8 in), usually smaller.
RANGE:	Central Amazon Basin and southern Central America.
NATURAL HABITAT:	Variety of (large) still and flowing waters.
WATER CONDITIONS:	Not critical. Temperature around 25°c (77°F).
DIET:	All foods, including some vegetable matter.
NOTES:	The generic name *Heros* has been proposed which, if accepted, will make *Cichlasoma* a synonym. This is a generally peaceful species which becomes aggressive during breeding. Eggs are laid on a prepared stone or piece of bogwood.

Festive Cichlid

Congo, **Convict** or **Zebra Cichlid**

Banded Cichlid, Severum

COMMON NAME:	**Blue Acara.**
SCIENTIFIC NAME:	*Aequidens pulcher.*
SYNONYM:	*Aequidens latifrons.*
SIZE:	18 cm (7 in).
RANGE:	Colombia, Panama, Trinidad, Venezuela.
NATURAL HABITAT:	Still and slow-moving waters.
WATER CONDITIONS:	Not critical but should not be allowed to become 'old'. Temperature 18–25°c (64.5–77°f).
DIET:	All foods.
NOTES:	Blue Acaras can be quite pugnacious, particularly with age. Eggs are usually laid on a stone. Eggs and fry are guarded by both parents.

COMMON NAME:	**Keyhole Cichlid.**
SCIENTIFIC NAME:	*Aequidens maronii.*
SYNONYM:	None.
SIZE:	10 cm (4 in).
RANGE:	Guiana, Guyana, Surinam.
NATURAL HABITAT:	No detailed accounts available – probably still and slow-moving waters.
WATER CONDITIONS:	Not critical but relatively soft, slightly acid water preferred. Temperature 20–28°c (68–82°f).
DIET:	All foods, particularly livefoods.
NOTES:	This is a shy, peaceful species. Eggs are laid on a pre-cleaned surface. Both parents guard the offspring.

COMMON NAME:	**Agassiz's Dwarf Cichlid.**
SCIENTIFIC NAME:	*Apistogramma agassizi.*
SYNONYM:	None.
SIZE:	About 7 cm (2.8 in).
RANGE:	Amazon Basin.
NATURAL HABITAT:	Shady waters.
WATER CONDITIONS:	Soft, slightly acid water. Temperature 17–19°c (62.5–66°f) in winter, 23–26°c (73.5–79°f) in summer.
DIET:	All foods, particularly livefoods.
NOTES:	Eggs usually laid in cavities. The female takes charge of the offspring and usually chases the male away after spawning. Other *Apistogramma* species kept include: *A. borellii* (sometimes referred to as *A. reitzigi*), *A. cacatuoides* and *A. steindachneri*.

Blue Acara

Keyhole Cichlid

Agassiz's Dwarf Cichlid

COMMON NAMES:	**Checkerboard** or **Chessboard Cichlid.**
SCIENTIFIC NAME:	*Crenicara filamentosa.*
SYNONYM:	None.
SIZE:	Around 8 cm (3.2 in).
RANGE:	Central Amazon Basin.
NATURAL HABITAT:	Shady waters with overhanging vegetation.
WATER CONDITIONS:	Relatively soft, slightly acid, *clean* water. Temperature 23–25°C (73.5–77°F).
DIET:	All foods.
NOTES:	This is a retiring, peaceful species which lays its eggs on stones or in cavities. Both parents guard the offspring.

COMMON NAMES:	**Ram, Butterfly Cichlid, Ramirez Dwarf Cichlid.**
SCIENTIFIC NAME:	*Papiliochromis ramirezi.*
SYNONYMS:	*Apistogramma ramirezi, Pseudoapistogramma ramirezi, Geophagus ramirezi, Microgeophagus ramirezi, Pseudogeophagus ramirezi.*
SIZE:	Around 5 cm (2 in).
RANGE:	Orinoco Basin.
NATURAL HABITAT:	Still and slow-flowing bodies of water with submerged vegetation.
WATER CONDITIONS:	Soft, acid water with regular partial changes. Temperature 23–25°C (73–77°F).
DIET:	Varied diet, to include livefoods.
NOTES:	There is also a golden form of this species. Rams are often timid and retiring but may become aggressive during spawning. Eggs are usually laid on a pre-cleaned stone. Both parents guard the eggs and fry.

COMMON NAME:	**Red-hump Geophagus.**
SCIENTIFIC NAME:	*Geophagus steindachneri.*
SYNONYMS:	*Geophagus hondae, G. magdalenae.*
SIZE:	Up to 12.5 cm (5 in).
RANGE:	Colombia (Río Cauca, Magdalena and Sinu Basins), Venezuela (Río Limon Basin).
NATURAL HABITAT:	Fast-flowing waters.
WATER CONDITIONS:	Not critical but clean, neutral, soft to moderately hard water has been found suitable. Temperature 25–27°C (77–80.5°F).
DIET:	All foods.
NOTES:	Males may be a bit aggressive towards each other but, on the whole, this is a peaceful mouthbrooding species which likes to sift sand in search of food (*Geophagus* means 'earth eater').

Checkerboard or **Chessboard Cichlid**

Ram, Butterfly Cichlid, Ramirez Dwarf Cichlid

Red-hump Geophagus

COMMON NAME:	**Orange Chromide.**
SCIENTIFIC NAME:	*Etroplus maculatus.*
SYNONYM:	None.
SIZE:	10 cm (4 in), maximum.
RANGE:	India, Sri Lanka.
NATURAL HABITAT:	Fresh and brackish estuarine reaches of rivers.
WATER CONDITIONS:	Will tolerate fresh (but not raw) water but prefers brackish or nearly marine conditions (one to two teaspoonfuls of salt per gallon). Temperature 21–26°C (70–79°F).
DIET:	All foods; should include vegetable matter.
NOTES:	A generally peaceful species. Eggs are laid on stones or in cavities. Both parents guard the offspring which may attach themselves to the adults' bodies at first.

COMMON NAME:	**Mozambique Mouthbrooder.**
SCIENTIFIC NAME:	*Oreochromis mossambicus.*
SYNONYMS:	*Sarotherodon mossambicus, Tilapia mossambica.*
SIZE:	Males up to 35 cm (13.8 in); females considerably smaller.
RANGE:	East Africa but introduced elsewhere as a food fish.
NATURAL HABITAT:	Variety of waters, usually with a partly sandy bottom.
WATER CONDITIONS:	Not critical. Temperature around 24°C (75°F).
DIET:	All foods.
NOTES:	*O. mossambicus* is a large, often aggressive species which will uproot plants and generally present considerable problems in smaller aquaria. It is, nevertheless, a beautiful, interesting mouthbrooder.

COMMON NAME:	**Jewel Cichlid.**
SCIENTIFIC NAME:	*Hemichromis bimaculatus* (see Notes).
SYNONYM:	None.
SIZE:	Around 12 cm (4.8 in).
RANGE:	Tropical Africa.
NATURAL HABITAT:	Still and flowing waters.
WATER CONDITIONS:	Not critical. Temperature around 25°C (77°F).
DIET:	All foods, particularly livefoods.
NOTES:	It is maintained, by at least one authority, that *H. bimaculatus* is, in fact, quite rare in aquaria and that most Jewel Cichlids kept are *H. guttatus*. Jewels are aggressive fish but excellent parents. Eggs are laid on stones or bogwood.

Orange Chromide

Mozambique Mouthbrooder

Jewel Cichlid

COMMON NAMES:	**Krib, Kribensis.**
SCIENTIFIC NAME:	*Pelvicachromis pulcher.*
SYNONYMS:	*Pelmatochromis kribensis, Pelmatochromis pulcher.*
SIZE:	Males up to 10 cm (4 in); females 7 cm (2.8 in).
RANGE:	Lower Nigeria.
NATURAL HABITAT:	Still and flowing waters.
WATER CONDITIONS:	Not critical (see Notes). Temperature 25–28°C (77–82°F).
DIET:	All foods.
NOTES:	Female plays leading role in breeding. Eggs are laid under shelter. Both parents guard eggs and young. Water chemistry may influence sex ratios of fry – higher pH values favouring females. This species becomes quite aggressive when breeding.

COMMON NAME:	**Golden Nyasa Cichlid.**
SCIENTIFIC NAME:	*Melanochromis auratus.*
SYNONYM:	*Pseudotropheus auratus.*
SIZE:	Around 11 cm (4.3 in).
RANGE:	Lake Malawi.
NATURAL HABITAT:	Near rocky shores.
WATER CONDITIONS:	Hard, alkaline water preferred. Temperature 22–25°C (71.5–77°F).
DIET:	All foods; should receive livefoods and vegetable matter.
NOTES:	This species can be aggressive, particularly the males. Eggs are brooded by the female in her mouth; she will also protect the fry for several weeks after hatching.

COMMON NAMES:	**Nyasa Blue** or **Zebra Cichlid.**
SCIENTIFIC NAME:	*Pseudotropheus zebra.*
SYNONYM:	None.
SIZE:	About 15 cm (6 in).
RANGE:	Lake Malawi.
NATURAL HABITAT:	Near rocky shores.
WATER CONDITIONS:	Hard, alkaline water preferred. Temperature 22–25°C (71.5–77°F).
DIET:	All foods; should receive livefoods and vegetable matter.
NOTES:	Numerous colour morphs (both natural and man-made) of this species exist. Recent findings suggest that some of the natural morphs may, in fact, be separate species. *P. zebra* is an aggressive mouthbrooder (the female being responsible for incubating the eggs and protecting the fry).

Krib, Kribensis

Golden Nyasa Cichlid

Nyasa Blue or **Zebra Cichlid**

COMMON NAMES:	**Blue Lumphead, Moorii.**
SCIENTIFIC NAME:	*Cyrtocara moorii.*
SYNONYM:	*Haplochromis moorii.*
SIZE:	Up to 20 cm (8 in).
RANGE:	Lake Malawi.
NATURAL HABITAT:	Over sandy beds.
WATER CONDITIONS:	Hard, alkaline water preferred. Temperature 20–25°c (68–77°f).
DIET:	All foods, particularly livefoods.
NOTES:	This is a generally peaceful species for its size but some individuals can be a bit unpredictable. Eggs are brooded orally by the female for up to four weeks, depending on temperature.

COMMON NAME:	**Lyretail Lamprologus.**
SCIENTIFIC NAME:	*Lamprologus brichardi.*
SYNONYM:	*Lamprologus savoryi elongatus.*
SIZE:	Around 10 cm (4 in).
RANGE:	Lake Tanganyika.
NATURAL HABITAT:	Clear, rocky beds down to a depth of 10 cm (33 ft).
WATER CONDITIONS:	Medium-hard to hard, alkaline water preferred. Temperature 23–28°c (73.5–82°f).
DIET:	Most foods; should receive some livefoods and vegetable matter.
NOTES:	Eggs laid in cavities. Both parents protect the offspring. *L. brichardi* can become aggressive towards members of their own species but are generally tolerant of other similarly sized fish.

COMMON NAMES:	**Masked Julidochromis, Masked Julie.**
SCIENTIFIC NAME:	*Julidochromis transcriptus.*
SYNONYM:	None.
SIZE:	Around 10 cm (4 in).
RANGE:	Lake Tanganyika.
NATURAL HABITAT:	Found among rock crevices.
WATER CONDITIONS:	Hard, alkaline water. Temperature 22–25°c (71.5–77°f).
DIET:	All foods; some vegetable matter should be provided from time to time.
NOTES:	Like other *Julidochromis* species, *J. transcriptus* is territorial and, therefore, aggressive towards intruders. Eggs are laid on the roofs of cavities. Both parents guard the eggs and fry.

Blue Lumphead, Moorii

Lyretail Lamprologus

Masked Julidochromis, Masked Julie

COMMON NAME:	**'Frontosa'.**
SCIENTIFIC NAME:	*Cyphotilapia frontosa.*
SYNONYM:	*Paratilapia frontosa.*
SIZE:	30 cm (12 in), usually smaller.
RANGE:	Lake Tanganyika.
NATURAL HABITAT:	Rocky beds down to a depth of 30 m (98 ft).
WATER CONDITIONS:	Hard, alkaline water. Temperature 22–28°C (71.5–82°F).
DIET:	All foods, particularly livefoods.
NOTES:	Despite its size, *C. frontosa* is generally a peaceful species. Spawning usually takes place in a cave but the eggs are brooded orally by the female for as long as three and a half weeks.

NB The mid-1970s and early 1980s saw a rapid expansion in the availability of African Rift Lake Cichlid species and varieties. While all benefit from hard alkaline conditions, size, temperature requirements and reproductive, dietary and other habits may differ significantly. No such species should, therefore, be bought without seeking advice from African Cichlid specialist hobbyists or dealers. Some old stalwarts, such as the Egyptian Mouthbrooder, *Pseudocrenilabrus multicolor* (formerly *Haplochromis multicolor*) have become relatively rare in the hobby with the upsurge of interest in Rift Lake Cichlids.

Family Anabantidae

COMMON NAMES:	**Climbing** or **Walking Perch.**
SCIENTIFIC NAME:	*Anabas testudineus.*
SYNONYMS:	*Anabas macrocephalus, A. scandens.*
SIZE:	Up to 25 cm (9.8 in), usually much smaller.
RANGE:	Southeast Asia.
NATURAL HABITAT:	Wide variety of waters.
WATER CONDITIONS:	Not critical. Temperature 15–30°C (59–86°F).
DIET:	All foods while young, predominantly livefood-based diet when mature.
NOTES:	The Climbing Perch neither climbs nor is a perch. Like other Anabantoids, they possess an auxiliary respiratory organ (labyrinth) which allows them to breathe directly from the air. Floating eggs are produced but no significant nest. Parental care only weakly developed. There is a rare xanthistic (yellow) form.

'Frontosa'

Climbing or **Walking Perch**

COMMON NAMES:	**Tail-spot Bush Fish, Climbing Perch.**
SCIENTIFIC NAME:	*Ctenopoma kingsleyae.*
SYNONYM:	None.
SIZE:	20 cm (8 in).
RANGE:	Coastal West Africa.
NATURAL HABITAT:	Quiet waters often densely vegetated.
WATER CONDITIONS:	Not critical. Temperature 23–28°C (73.5–82°F).
DIET:	All foods when young, predominantly livefood-based diet when mature.
NOTES:	Floating eggs are produced but given no parental protection. *C. kingsleyae* is aggressive, active and a free-spawner. Other free-spawning Bush Fish include *C. acutirostre, C. oxyrhynchus, C. ocellatum* and *C. multispinis.* Bubblenesters include *C. fasciolatum, C. ansorgei, C. nanum* and *C. damasii.* All are predatory but not necessarily as aggressive as *C. kingsleyae.*

Family Belontiidae

COMMON NAMES:	**Comb-tail or Comb-tail Paradise Fish.**
SCIENTIFIC NAME:	*Belontia signata.*
SYNONYM:	None.
SIZE:	Up to 13 cm (5 in).
RANGE:	Sri Lanka.
NATURAL HABITAT:	Still, vegetated waters but capable of colonising new habitats.
WATER CONDITIONS:	Not critical. Temperature around 25°C (77°F).
DIET:	All foods, particularly livefoods.
NOTES:	Eggs are laid in a male-built bubblenest. Eggs and fry are protected for several days by the male. *B. signata* is a retiring fish with predatory habits, as is *B. hasselti* (the Honeycomb Comb-tail) from Borneo, Java, Malaysia and Sumatra.

COMMON NAME:	**Paradise Fish.**
SCIENTIFIC NAME:	*Macropodus opercularis.*
SYNONYM:	*Labrus opercularis.*
SIZE:	Around 9 cm (3.5 in).
RANGE:	Eastern China, Korea, South Vietnam.
NATURAL HABITAT:	Variety of waters.
WATER CONDITIONS:	Not critical. Temperature: extremely wide range; may be kept in unheated aquaria.
DIET:	All foods.
NOTES:	One of the very first tropical species kept in Europe. *M. opercularis* can be very aggressive. It is a bubblenester with brooding duties carried out by the male. An albino and a dark form (the Black Paradise Fish – often referred to as *M. opercularis concolor*) are also available.

Tail-spot Bush Fish, Climbing Perch

Comb-tail or **Comb-tail Paradise Fish**

Paradise Fish

COMMON NAME:	**Spike-tailed Paradise Fish.**
SCIENTIFIC NAMES:	(i) *Macropodus cupanus cupanus*; (ii) *Macropodus cupanus dayi*.
SYNONYMS:	*Polyacanthus cupanus, Macropodus dayi, Polyacanthus dayi*.
SIZE:	Around 7 cm (2.8 in).
RANGE:	(i) Coastal areas of India and Sri Lanka; (ii) Burma, Sri Lanka, Sumatra, Vietnam.
NATURAL HABITAT:	Variety of waters (including brackish waters).
WATER CONDITIONS:	Not critical. Temperature 18–25°C (64.5–77°F).
DIET:	All foods.
NOTES:	Both subspecies are tolerant of other fish. Males build bubblenests at the surface or under a leaf and undertake brooding responsibilities.

COMMON NAMES:	**Siamese Fighting Fish, Fighter.**
SCIENTIFIC NAME:	*Betta splendens*.
SYNONYM:	See Notes.
SIZE:	Around 6 cm (2.5 in).
RANGE:	Far East.
NATURAL HABITAT:	Variety of waters, usually still or very slow-flowing.
WATER CONDITIONS:	Not critical. Temperature 24–28°C (75–82°F).
DIET:	All foods.
NOTES:	Males are very aggressive towards each other and (often) towards females, but are tolerant of other species. *B. splendens* is the classic bubblenester. Numerous colour and fin varieties of domesticated fighters exist.

Some Unusual Bettas Which Are Occasionally Available

Scientific Name	Reproductive Strategy	Notes
B. bellica	Bubblenester	Slender Betta
B. brederi	Mouthbrooder	Probably a form of *B. pugnax*
B. coccina	Bubblenester	Red Fighting Fish
B. fasciata	Bubblenester	Striped Fighting Fish
B. imbellis	Bubblenester	Beautiful, Crescent or Peaceful Fighting Fish
B. macrostoma	Mouthbrooder	Brunei Beauty
B. picta	Mouthbrooder	Probably incorporates *B. rubra, taeniata* and *trifasciata*
B. pugnax	Mouthbrooder	Penang Betta
B. rubra	Mouthbrooder	Probably synonymous with *B. picta*
B. smaragdina	Bubblenester	Emerald Fighting Fish
B. taeniata	Mouthbrooder	Striped Betta. Probably synonymous with *B. picta*
B. trifasciata	Mouthbrooder	Probably synonymous with *B. picta* or *B. taeniata*
B. unimaculata	Mouthbrooder	One-spot Betta

The situation concerning the naming of the various Bettas is in a somewhat confused state at the time of writing. A reclassification based on reproductive strategy has not yet received universal acceptance. If it does, generic names such as *Pseudobetta* and *Parophiocephalus* may appear in the literature. All the above-mentioned Bettas may be maintained at around 25°C (77°F) or slightly higher. Many species are aggressive towards their own kind to varying degrees.

Spike-tailed Paradise Fish

Siamese Fighting Fish, male and female

Emerald Fighting Fish

COMMON NAME:	**Dwarf Gourami.**
SCIENTIFIC NAME:	*Colisa lalia.*
SYNONYM:	None in recent aquarium literature.
SIZE:	Males around 5 cm (2 in); females usually smaller.
RANGE:	India, particularly Assam and Bengal.
NATURAL HABITAT:	Still waters.
WATER CONDITIONS:	Not critical. Temperature 24–28°C (75–82°F).
DIET:	All foods.
NOTES:	There are several man-made varieties of this species, e.g. Sunset, Neon and Blue. Males build beautiful bubblenests at the surface. Brooding of eggs and fry (for several days) is undertaken by males.

Other *Colisa* Species Usually Available

Common Name	Scientific Name	Size cm (in)	Habits
Honey or Honey Dwarf Gourami	*C. chuna*	5 (2) max.	Shy, retiring but beautiful species during breeding
Giant, Indian, Striped or Banded Gourami	*C. fasciata*	Around 10 (3.9)	Males become aggressive at spawning time
Thick-lipped Gourami	*C. labiosa*	Around 8 (3.2)	As for *C. fasciata*

All the above species are bubblenesters with requirements similar to *Colisa lalia. C. labiosa* and *C. fasciata* can interbreed and produce fertile hybrids. It is possible, therefore, that they may be more closely related than their specific status suggests. Hybrids between *C. lalia* and *C. labiosa* all (eventually) end up as males.

Other *Trichogaster* Species Usually Available

Common Name	Scientific Name	Size cm (in)	Habits
Lace, Mosaic or Pearl Gourami	*T. leeri*	Around 10 (3.9)	Generally more peaceful than *T. trichopterus*
Moonlight or Thin-lipped Gourami	*T. microlepis*	Around 15 (5.9)	Males may tear plants and incorporate them in their bubblenests
Snakeskin Gourami	*T. pectoralis*	Around 25 (9.8)	Generally placid

All the above are bubblenesters with requirements similar to *Trichogaster trichopterus.*

COMMON NAMES:	**Two-Spot, Three-Spot, Blue, Opaline (Cosby), Amethyst, Lavender, Brown, Golden** or **Platinum Gourami.**
SCIENTIFIC NAME:	*Trichogaster trichopterus.*
SYNONYM:	*T. trichopterus sumatranus* (for Blue variety).
SIZE:	Up to 15 cm (6 in), usually smaller.
RANGE:	Great Sunda Islands, Malaya, South Vietnam, Sumatra (possibly) and Thailand. (This applies only to the Two/Three-Spot and, perhaps, Blue/ Lavender/Brown types – all the others are man-made varieties).
NATURAL HABITAT:	Jungle streams.
WATER CONDITIONS:	Not critical. Temperature 23–28°C (73–82°F).
DIET:	All foods.
NOTES:	Males can become aggressive even outside the breeding season. All varieties will interbreed. Bubblenest is constructed by the male who undertakes brooding responsibilities until fry are free-swimming.

Dwarf Gourami

Thick-lipped Gourami

Two-spot, Three-spot or **Blue Gourami**

COMMON NAME: **Pigmy Gourami** (see Notes).

SCIENTIFIC NAME: *Trichopsis pumilus.*

SYNONYM: *Ctenops pumilus.*

SIZE: Around 3.5 cm (1.5 in).

RANGE: From Java northwards to Indo China.

NATURAL HABITAT: Densely vegetated jungle streams.

WATER CONDITIONS: Preferably soft and slightly acid but other conditions will also be tolerated. Temperature 25–28°c (77–82°F).

DIET: All foods, particularly small livefoods.

NOTES: Other names occasionally used for this peaceful species are the Sparkling Gourami (usually reserved for *Trichopsis schalleri*) and the Dwarf Gourami (normally applied to *Colisa lalia*). *T. pumilus, T. schalleri* and *T. vittatus* are bubblenesters collectively known as Croaking Gouramis owing to the sounds they make, particularly during courtship and aggression.

Family Helostomatidae

COMMON NAME: **Kissing Gourami.**

SCIENTIFIC NAME: *Helostoma temmincki.*

SYNONYM: *Helostoma rudolfi.*

SIZE: Up to 30 cm (12 in), usually smaller.

RANGE: Borneo, Greater Sunda Islands, Malaya, Thailand.

NATURAL HABITAT: Variety of waters.

WATER CONDITIONS: Not critical. Temperature 25–30°c (77–86°F).

DIET: All foods. A regular vegetable component must be provided.

NOTES: The kissing behaviour for which this fish is famous is linked to aggression rather than affection. Even so, *H. temmincki* is generally peaceful and tolerant of other species. It is available in 'wild' (Green) and Pink forms and has only rarely been bred in aquaria.

Some Other Anabantoids Kept in Aquaria

Common Name	Scientific Name	Family	Size cm (in)	Water Conditions	Diet and Habits
Ornate Paradise Fish, Mottled Pointed tailed Gourami or Kretser's Dwarf Macropod	*Malpulutta kretseri*	Belontiidae	6 (2.4)	Soft and acid. 25°c (77°F) and above	Mostly small livefoods. Shy and retiring
Chocolate Gourami	*Sphaerichthys osphromenoides*	Belontiidae	5 (2)	As above	As above

Pigmy Gourami

Kissing Gourami

Common Name	Scientific Name	Family	Size cm (in)	Water Conditions	Diet and Habits
Liquorice Gourami or Deissner's Dwarf Macropod	*Parosphromenus deissneri*	Belontiidae	4 (1.6)	As above	Mostly small livefoods. Shy and retiring
Giant Gourami or Goramy	*Osphronemus goramy*	Osphronemidae	60 (23.6)	Not critical. 20–30°C (68–86°F)	All foods. Robust and active

None of the above fish is easy to keep in peak condition for prolonged periods (the easiest being *O. goramy*). However, since these species do become available within the hobby, they warrant inclusion, particularly to make the point that specialist advice and literature should be sought by anyone contemplating keeping them.

Family Nandidae

COMMON NAMES:	**Badis, Chameleon Fish.**
SCIENTIFIC NAME:	*Badis badis.*
SYNONYM:	None.
SIZE:	Males up to 8 cm (3.2 in); females 6 cm (2.5 in).
RANGE:	Southeast Asia.
NATURAL HABITAT:	Still waters.
WATER CONDITIONS:	Not critical. Temperature around 25° c (77° F).
DIET:	All foods, which should include livefoods.
NOTES:	*Badis* is thought by some ichthyologists to be sufficiently different to the other Nandids (mostly Leaf Fishes) to warrant their separation into a separate family, the Badidae. Close affinities with Anabantoids are also thought to exist. *B. badis* is not generally an aggressive species. Eggs are laid in a cave and are guarded by the male until they hatch and the fry become free-swimming.

Family Callichthyidae

COMMON NAMES:	**Emerald** or **Short-bodied Catfish.**
SCIENTIFIC NAME:	*Brochis splendens.*
SYNONYM:	*Brochis coeruleus.*
SIZE:	Males around 7.5 cm (3 in); females 9 cm (3.5 in).
RANGE:	Brazil, Ecuador, Peru.
NATURAL HABITAT:	Slow-flowing waters, often with heavily vegetated banks.
WATER CONDITIONS:	Not critical. Temperature 24–27° c (75–80.5° F).
DIET:	Most foods, particularly worms.
NOTES:	Eggs are deposited on plants or sides of the aquarium. No brooding behaviour is exhibited by either parent. This is a peaceful species.

COMMON NAMES:	**Bronze Catfish, Bronze Corydoras.**
SCIENTIFIC NAME:	*Corydoras aeneus.*
SYNONYM:	None.
SIZE:	Around 7.5 cm (3 in).
RANGE:	Widely distributed in South America.
NATURAL HABITAT:	Slow-flowing, clear waters.
WATER CONDITIONS:	Not critical, but neutral to slightly alkaline water seems to be preferred. Temperature 18–26° c (64.5–79° F).
DIET:	All foods, particularly worms.
NOTES:	Eggs are carried by the female for a while between her cupped pelvic fins (which act as a pouch) and deposited on plants or other surfaces. The wild-type colour pattern is variable; an albino (man-made) form is also available. This is a peaceful species.

Badis, **Chameleon Fish**

Emerald or **Short-bodied Catfish**

Bronze Catfish, **Bronze Corydoras**

COMMON NAMES:	**Peppered Catfish, Peppered Corydoras.**
SCIENTIFIC NAME:	*Corydoras palaeatus.*
SYNONYM:	None.
SIZE:	7.5 cm (3 in).
RANGE:	Northern Argentina and southern Brazil.
NATURAL HABITAT:	Flowing waters.
WATER CONDITIONS:	Not critical but extremes of pH must be avoided. Temperature 18–23°c (64.5–73.5°F).
DIET:	All foods, particularly worms.
NOTES:	Breeding behaviour is similar to *C. aeneus.* Other shared characteristics are variable wild-type colour patterns, a man-made albino form, and a peaceful disposition.

COMMON NAMES:	**Armoured** or **Bubblenest-building Catfish.**
SCIENTIFIC NAME:	*Callichthys callichthys.*
SYNONYM:	None.
SIZE:	20 cm (8 in), usually smaller.
RANGE:	Widely distributed in tropical South America.
NATURAL HABITAT:	Shallow still waters, often with densely vegetated banks.
WATER CONDITIONS:	Not critical. Temperature 24–26°c (75–79°F).
DIET:	All foods, particularly worms.
NOTES:	Eggs are laid in a bubblenest built by the male who guards them until they hatch. *Callichthys* may be distinguished from the very similar *Hoplosternum* species by its smaller eyes and rounded caudal fin.

Some Other *Corydoras* Species Found in Aquaria

Common Name	Scientific Name	Size cm (in)	Water Conditions	Diet and Habits
Blacktop Corydoras	*C. acutus*	5.3 (2.1)	Soft, slightly acid water; 23–27°c (73.5–80.5°F)	All foods, particularly worms. Peaceful
Arched, Skunk or Tabatinga Corydoras	*C. arcuatus*	5 (2)	Neutral to slightly alkaline water; 22–26°c (71.5–79°F)	As above
Elegant Corydoras	*C. elegans*	6 (2.4)	As for *C. arcuatus*	As above
Dwarf Corydoras	*C. habrosus*	3 (1.2)	Not critical; 23–26°c (73.5–79°F)	As above
Dwarf or Pygmy Corydoras	*C. hastatus*	2 (0.8)	As for *C. habrosus*	As above
Leopard Corydoras	*C. julii*	6 (2.4)	Not critical; 20–26°c (68–79°F)	As above

Peppered Catfish, Peppered Corydoras

Armoured or **Bubblenest-building Catfish**

Common Name	Scientific Name	Size cm (in)	Water Conditions	Diet and Habits
Bandit or Masked Corydoras	*C. metae*	6 (2.4)	Not critical; 23–29°c (73.5–84°F)	All foods, particularly worms. Peaceful
Myer's Corydoras	*C. myersi**	6 (2.4)	Neutral to slightly alkaline; 24–28°c (75–82°F)	As above
Blue Corydoras	*C. nattereri*	6 (2.4)	Not critical; 18–22°c (64.5–71.5°F)	As above
Network or Reticulated Corydoras	*C. reticulatus*	7 (2.75)	Neutral to slightly alkaline; 20–26°c (68–79°F)	As above

Note *There is considerable confusion over the correct scientific name of Myer's Catfish. It has been suggested that *C. myersi* is synonymous with *C. rabauti* or (perhaps more correctly) *C. zygatus*.

131

Family Siluridae

COMMON NAMES:	**Glass Catfish, Ghost Fish.**
SCIENTIFIC NAME:	*Kryptopterus bicirrhus.*
SYNONYM:	None.
SIZE:	12 cm (4.7 in).
RANGE:	Borneo, Java, Sumatra, Thailand.
NATURAL HABITAT:	Running waters (often found in the shade).
WATER CONDITIONS:	Not critical as long as the water is well-oxygenated. Temperature around 26°c (79°F).
DIET:	Will accept dry foods but should receive a regular supply of livefoods.
NOTES:	This is a midwater, crepuscular (twilight) species best kept in shoals. No reports of successful spawning in aquaria are available.

Family Mochokidae

COMMON NAME:	**Upside-down Catfish.**
SCIENTIFIC NAME:	*Synodontis nigriventris.*
SYNONYM:	None.
SIZE:	Around 7.5 cm (3 in).
RANGE:	Zaire Basin.
NATURAL HABITAT:	Variety of waters.
WATER CONDITIONS:	Not critical. Temperature 22–26°c (71.5–79°F).
DIET:	Livefoods and vegetation.
NOTES:	As the common name implies, this peaceful species frequently swims upside-down. Other *Synodontis* species also do this but less regularly. *S. nigriventris* has been spawned in aquaria but no detailed accounts are available.

Family Loricariidae

COMMON NAMES:	**Pleco** or **Plecostomus.**
SCIENTIFIC NAME:	*Hypostomus plecostomus.*
SYNONYM:	*Plecostomus* spp
SIZE:	Up to 45 cm (18 in) but usually much smaller.
RANGE:	South America, particularly Guiana, Guyana, Surinam and Venezuela.
NATURAL HABITAT:	Clear, fast-flowing waters.
WATER CONDITIONS:	Not critical. Temperature 20–25°c (68–77°F).
DIET:	Most foods but these must include vegetable matter.
NOTES:	There is still some confusion regarding the classification of this and closely related species, e.g. *H. punctatus.* Plecos have (rarely) been spawned in aquaria – the eggs are laid in cavities and protected by one of the parents.

Glass Catfish, Ghost Fish

Upside-down Catfish

Pleco, Plecostomus

133

COMMON NAME: **Whiptail Catfish.**

SCIENTIFIC NAME: *Rineloricaria parva.*

SYNONYM: *Loricaria parva.*

SIZE: Around 12 cm (4.7 in).

RANGE: Paraguay.

NATURAL HABITAT: Flowing waters.

WATER CONDITIONS: Relatively acid water. Temperature 21–28°C (70–82°F).

DIET: Predominantly vegetarian but can include some live and flaked foods.

NOTES: Eggs usually laid on wood and cared for by the male. Sexual dimorphism is apparent in *Rineloricaria* with males possessing bristles on the head, cheek and pectoral fins.

Whiptail Catfish

Angelica Pim

Family Pimelodidae

COMMON NAME:	**Angelica Pim.**
SCIENTIFIC NAME:	*Pimelodus pictus.*
SYNONYM:	*Pimelodella pictus.*
SIZE:	Around 11 cm (4.3 in).
RANGE:	Colombia, Peru.
NATURAL HABITAT:	Variety of waters.
WATER CONDITIONS:	Neutral to slightly alkaline. Temperature 22–25°C (71.5–77°F).
DIET:	Livefoods preferred.
NOTES:	This is a predominantly nocturnal species (although also active during the day) with some predatory habits. It should, therefore, not be kept with small fish. No details of aquarium spawnings are available.

Some Other Catfishes Kept in Aquaria

Common Name	Scientific Name	Family	Size cm (in)	Water Conditions	Diet and Habits
Banjo or Frying Pan Catfish	*Bunocephalus* spp	Aspredinidae (Bunocepha-lidae)	Approx. 8 (3.2)	Not critical. Around 24°C (75°F)	Most foods. Nocturnal bottom scavenger
Giraffe-nosed Catfish	*Auchenoglanis occidentalis*	Bagridae	50 (19.7)	Not critical; 24–28°C (75–82°F)	Predatory
Port-hole Catfish	*Dianema longibarbis*	Callichthyidae	12 (4.7)	Not critical; 24°C (75°F)	Most foods. Peaceful
Stripe-tailed Catfish	*Dianema urostriata*	Calichthyidae	As above	As above	As above
Walking Catfish	*Clarias batrachus*	Clariidae	60 (23.6)	Not critical; 20–25°C (68–77°F)	Predatory
Channel Catfish	*Ictalurus punctatus*	Ictaluridae	Around 80 (31.5)	Not critical; as low as 18°C (65°F)	As above
Bristle-nosed Catfish	*Ancistrus* spp	Loricariidae	Around 14 (5.5)	Not critical, but clean; 25°C (77°F)	Predominantly vegetarian. Peaceful
Midget Sucker Catfish	*Otocinclus affinis*	Loricariidae	5 (2)	Soft slightly acid, 21–29°C (70–84°F)	As above
Polka-dot African Catfish	*Synodontis angelicus*	Mochokidae	19 (7.5)	Neutral to slightly acid and soft; 22–29°C (71.5–84°F)	Most foods, including worms and vegetable matter. Generally peaceful
Siamese Shark, Smoky Glass Catfish	*Pangasius sutchi*	Pangasiidae	Around 17 (6.7)	Not critical; 24°C (75°F)	Livefoods preferred. Relatively peaceful with similarly sized fish but will eat small fish
Slender Pim	*Pimelodella cristata (P. gracilis)*	Pimelodidae	Up to around 25 (9.8)	Not critical; 24–27°C (75–80.5°F)	Livefoods. Nocturnal and quite peaceful but will eat small fish

Family Gyrinocheilidae

COMMON NAMES:	**Sucking Loach, Chinese Algae Eater.**
SCIENTIFIC NAME:	*Gyrinocheilus aymonieri.*
SYNONYM:	None.
SIZE:	Up to 25 cm (9.8 in) in the wild – usually much smaller.
RANGE:	Thailand.
NATURAL HABITAT:	Clear, well-oxygenated flowing mountain streams.
WATER CONDITIONS:	Not critical but well-aerated, slightly alkaline water preferred. Temperature 21–30°C (70–86°F).
DIET:	Predominantly vegetarian but will accept some other foods.
NOTES:	This is a very fast-swimming species. Some specimens can become aggressive and may scrape off body mucus from the body surface of slower swimming species. Unusual gill arrangement allows Sucking Loaches to attach themselves, feed and breathe simultaneously.

Family Cobitidae

COMMON NAME:	**Myer's Loach, Slimy Myersi.**
SCIENTIFIC NAME:	*Acanthophthalmus myersi* (see Notes).
SYNONYM:	See Notes.
SIZE:	Up to 8 cm (3 in).
RANGE:	Thailand.
NATURAL HABITAT:	Shallow, flowing waters with sandy bottoms.
WATER CONDITIONS:	Not critical but should be clean. Temperature 24–30°C (75–86°F).
DIET:	Bottom-living livefoods preferred but other foods will also be accepted.
NOTES:	There is considerable debate concerning the number of species and/or subspecies of *Acanthophthalmus*. Patterns are variable but these seem to be valid: *A. kuhli, A. javanicus, A. myersi, A. semicinctus* and *A. shelfordi*.

COMMON NAME:	**Clown Loach.**
SCIENTIFIC NAME:	*Botia macracantha.*
SYNONYM:	None.
SIZE:	20 cm (8 in) – usually smaller.
RANGE:	Borneo, Indonesia, Sumatra.
NATURAL HABITAT:	Still and slow-flowing waters.
WATER CONDITIONS:	Not critical but soft, acid water seems to be preferred. Raw water must be avoided. Temperature 23–26°C (73.5–79°F).
DIET:	Bottom-living livefoods are preferred but other foods will be taken.
NOTES:	This is a shoaling species which, unlike most other Botias, is active during the day. Breeding has been achieved in aquaria.

Sucking Loach, Chinese Algae Eater

Myer's Loach, Slimy Myersi

Clown Loach

Some Other *Botia* Species Found in Aquaria

Common Name	Scientific Name	Size cm (in)	Water Conditions	Diet and Habits
Beaufort's Loach	*B. beauforti*	Around 20 (7.9)	Soft, slightly acid and well-aerated; 23–26°c (73.5–79°F)	Bottom-living livefoods, plus dry foods. Non-shoaling, generally peaceful, twilight/nocturnal species
Hora's, Mouse or Skunk Loach	*B. horae*	9 (3.5)	As above	A shoaling species – otherwise as above
Banded Loach	*B. hymenophysa*	Around 15 (5.9)	Soft, slightly acid and well-aerated; 24–27°c (75–80.5°F)	Bottom-living livefoods and small fish. Non-shoaling, twilight/nocturnal species
Pakistani or Reticulated Loach	*B. lohachata*	11 (4.3)	As above	As for *B. horae*
Orange-finned Loach	*B. modesta*	19 (7.5)	As above	As above
Chain or Dwarf Loach	*B. sidthimunki*	5.5 (2.1)	Soft to slightly hard and well-aerated; 23–26°c (73.5–79°F)	As above but also quite active during the day
Zebra Loach	*B. striata*	8.5 (3.3)	Soft, slightly acid and well-aerated; 20–25°c (68–77°F)	As for *B. horae*

Family Cyprinodontidae

Explanatory Notes Traditionally, all Killi-fishes (Egglaying Toothcarps) have been classified in the family Cyprinodontidae. However, several modifications were proposed by Parenti in her revision of Cyprinodontiform fishes, including live-bearers, in 1981 (see Bibliography). As a result, some of the common genera of Killies may begin to appear under different families in years to come. For example:

Lyretail, Lyretailed Panchax

New (Proposed) Family	Some Genera
Aplocheilidae	*Epiplatys, Pachypanchax, Aplocheilus, Aphyosemion, Nothobranchius.*
Rivulidae	*Rivulus, Cynolebias, Rachovia.*
Poeciliidae	*Aplocheilichthys* (same family as Guppies, Swordtails, etc.).
Valenciidae	*Valencia.*
Cyprinodontidae	*Aphanius, Cyprinodon, Orestias, Jordanella.*

Killifish can be grouped as follows:

1. **Annuals** – live in areas where bodies of water dry up every year. Eggs are laid in the mud and hatch out when the rains return.

2. **Semi-annuals** – live in areas where bodies of water may not dry out. Some species may act as non-annuals, depending on environmental conditions.

3. **Non-annuals** – live in permanent bodies of water and may survive for several years.

In aquarium terms, breeding strategies are divided into:

1. Mop-spawners – eggs are laid among vegetation or spawning mops.

2. Substrate spawners – eggs are laid in the bottom of the tank (usually in peat).

On the whole, Killifish are best kept in a tank of their own.

Some Species of Killifish Suitable for Beginners

Annuals	Semi-annuals	Non-annuals
Aphyosemion filamentosum	Aphyosemion armieti	Aphyosemion ahli
A. robertsoni	A. gardneri	A. striatum
Cynolebias nigripinnis	A. gulare	Aplocheilus lineatus
C. whitei	A. marmoratum	Epiplatys bifasciatus
Nothobranchius foerschi	A. ndianum	E. roloffi
N. rachovi	A. puerlzi	Pachypanchax playfairii

COMMON NAMES:	**Lyretail, Lyretailed Panchax.**
SCIENTIFIC NAME:	*Aphyosemion australe.*
SYNONYM:	*Aphyosemion polychromum*
SIZE:	6.5 cm (2.6 in).
RANGE:	Gabon, southern Cameroun.
NATURAL HABITAT:	Coastal standing waters.
WATER CONDITIONS:	Soft, acid water, preferably peat-stained. Temperature 18–24°c (64.5–75°F).
DIET:	Livefoods, plus some dry foods.
NOTES:	Several varieties are available, including an orange or reddish-gold one. This species is a non-annual mop-spawner – eggs take around two weeks to hatch.

COMMON NAME:	**Argentine Pearl.**
SCIENTIFIC NAME:	*Cynolebias bellotti.*
SYNONYM:	None.
SIZE:	Around 5 cm (2 in).
RANGE:	Río Plata Basin (Argentina).
NATURAL HABITAT:	Seasonal ponds, ditches and other bodies of standing water.
WATER CONDITIONS:	Soft, acid water which should be changed regularly. Temperature 15–22°C (59–71.5°F).
DIET:	Livefoods, but will also accept dry foods.
NOTES:	Males are often aggressive towards each other. This is a typical annual substrate spawner. Eggs must be stored in damp peat for several months, inspected with a magnifying glass occasionally and placed in water when the embryos are fully developed.

COMMON NAMES:	**Clown Killi, Comet Panchax.**
SCIENTIFIC NAME:	*Epiplatys annulatus.*
SYNONYM:	*Pseudoepiplatys annulatus.*
SIZE:	Around 3 cm (1.2 in).
RANGE:	West Africa (Sierra Leone to Liberia).
NATURAL HABITAT:	Still and slow-moving waters with vegetated banks.
WATER CONDITIONS:	Soft and acid. Temperature 23–26°C (73.5–79°F).
DIET:	Small livefoods but some dry foods may also be accepted.
NOTES:	This is a peaceful species best kept on its own. It is a typical non-annual mop-spawner – eggs take about a fortnight to develop.

COMMON NAME:	**Guenther's Nothobranch.**
SCIENTIFIC NAME:	*Nothobranchius guentheri.*
SYNONYM:	None.
SIZE:	6.5 cm (2.6 in).
RANGE:	East Africa.
NATURAL HABITAT:	Seasonal pools and other bodies of standing water.
WATER CONDITIONS:	Soft and slightly acid. Temperature 23–26°C (73.5–79°F).
DIET:	Livefoods but some dry foods may also be accepted.
NOTES:	This species is intolerant of others. It is a typical annual substrate spawner (see *Cynolebias bellotti*) – incubation period four to six weeks.

Argentine Pearl

Clown Killi, Comet Panchax

Guenther's Nothobranch

COMMON NAME:	**American Flag Fish.**
SCIENTIFIC NAME:	*Jordanella floridae.*
SYNONYM:	None.
SIZE:	Around 6 cm (2.5 in).
RANGE:	Florida, Yucatán and southwards to Belize.
NATURAL HABITAT:	Variety of standing waters.
WATER CONDITIONS:	Not critical but slightly alkaline water is sometimes recommended. Temperature 19–25° c (66–76° F).
DIET:	Livefoods and vegetable matter but will also accept dry foods.
NOTES:	Males are often aggressive towards each other. Eggs are laid on plants or near the bottom. Brooding responsibilities during embryonic development (five to six days) are carried out by the males.

Family Oryziatidae
(see *Notes*)

COMMON NAMES:	**Geisha-girl** or **Japanese Medaka, Rice Fish.**
SCIENTIFIC NAME:	*Oryzias latipes.*
SYNONYM:	None.
SIZE:	Around 4 cm (1.5 in).
RANGE:	Japan.
NATURAL HABITAT:	Small streams and rice paddies.
WATER CONDITIONS:	Around neutral. Temperature: extremely wide range – from less than 15° c (59° F) to more than 28° c (82° F).
DIET:	Live and dry foods accepted.
NOTES:	Some classifications group the Medakas with the Killifishes. There are three main varieties: the wild type, a golden one and an 'unreliable' red one. This peaceful species is unusual in that the females carry the eggs attached to their vent until they find a suitable substrate on which to deposit them (usually fine-leaved vegetation). Other species of *Oryzias* kept in aquaria are *O. celebensis* and *O. javanicus*.

Family Atherinidae

COMMON NAME:	**Madagascan Rainbow.**
SCIENTIFIC NAME:	*Bedotia geayi.*
SYNONYM:	None.
SIZE:	Around 10 cm (4 in).
RANGE:	Malagasy.
NATURAL HABITAT:	Wide variety of waters.
WATER CONDITIONS:	Not critical. Temperature around 25° c (77° F).
DIET:	Live and dried foods accepted.
NOTES:	*Bedotia* is a mop-spawner (a characteristic shared by some Killifish). Eggs take about 10 days to hatch, depending on temperature.

American Flag Fish

Geisha-girl or **Japanese Medaka, Rice Fish**

Madagascan Rainbow

COMMON NAMES:	**Celebes Rainbow** or **Sailfish.**
SCIENTIFIC NAME:	*Telmatherina ladigesi.*
SYNONYM:	None.
SIZE:	7 cm (2.8 in).
RANGE:	Borneo, Sulawesi (Celebes).
NATURAL HABITAT:	Freshwater lakes.
WATER CONDITIONS:	Composition not critical but very hard water and abrupt changes must be avoided. Temperature 24–26°C (75–79°F).
DIET:	Surface livefoods, e.g. fruitflies, are preferred.
NOTES:	Breeding habits are as for *Bedotia geayi.*

Family Melanotaeniidae
(see *Notes*)

COMMON NAMES:	**Australian, Black-lined** or **Dwarf Rainbowfish.**
SCIENTIFIC NAME:	*Melanotaenia maccullochi.*
SYNONYM:	None.
SIZE:	Around 9 cm (3.5 in).
RANGE:	Northeastern Australia.
NATURAL HABITAT:	Well-oxygenated flowing waters.
WATER CONDITIONS:	Not critical. Temperature 22–25°C (71.5–77°F).
DIET:	Live and dried foods accepted.
NOTES:	Some authorities classify *Melanotaenia* in the Atherinidae, along with *Bedotia* and *Telmatherina*. Greenwood and others place this genus, along with five other genera, in the Melanotaeniidae (see Bibliography). Spawning is as in *Bedotia* – alternatively, fine-leaved vegetation may be used instead of mops. The number of species of *Melanotaenia* becoming available has been increasing for some years.

Family Gasteropelecidae

COMMON NAME:	**Silver Hatchetfish.**
SCIENTIFIC NAME:	*Gasteropelecus levis* (see Notes).
SYNONYM:	None.
SIZE:	Around 6 cm (2.5 in).
RANGE:	Lower reaches of the Amazon.
NATURAL HABITAT:	Still and slow-flowing bodies of water.
WATER CONDITIONS:	Soft, peaty water. Temperature 23–28°C (73.5–82°F).
DIET:	Livefoods are preferred.
NOTES:	*G. levis* is very similar to the Common Hatchetfish, *G. sternicla*. Other species available, to a greater or lesser extent, include *G. maculatus* (Spotted Hatchetfish), *Carnegiella marthae* (Black-winged Hatchetfish) and *C. strigata* (Marbled Hatchetfish). All have similar requirements. Some species have been bred in aquaria but no detailed reports are available.

Celebes Rainbow, Sailfish

Australian, Black-lined or **Dwarf Rainbowfish**

Silver Hatchetfish

Family Centropomidae (Formerly Ambassidae)

COMMON NAME:	**Indian Glass Fish.**
SCIENTIFIC NAME:	*Chanda ranga.*
SYNONYM:	*Ambassis lala.*
SIZE:	Around 6 cm (2.5 in).
RANGE:	Burma, India, Thailand.
NATURAL HABITAT:	Brackish estuaries or coastal waters.
WATER CONDITIONS:	Hard, alkaline water with up to two or three teaspoonfuls of salt per gallon. Temperature around 25°C (77°F).
DIET:	Livefoods are preferred.
NOTES:	On the whole, this is a timid species. Eggs are scattered near the surface and stick to plants. Adults should be removed when the fry hatch.

Family Gobiidae

COMMON NAMES:	**Bumblebee, Golden Banded Goby.**
SCIENTIFIC NAME:	*Brachygobius* spp (see Notes).
SYNONYM:	See Notes.
SIZE:	Around 4.5 cm (1.8 in).
RANGE:	Far East.
NATURAL HABITAT:	Fresh, brackish and (*B. aggregatus*) marine waters.
WATER CONDITIONS:	Although freshwater is tolerated, Bumblebees are best kept in hard, alkaline water with one or two teaspoonfuls of salt per gallon. Temperature 24–26°C (76–79°F).
DIET:	Livefoods preferred.
NOTES:	The various *Brachygobius* species are very difficult to identify. Those found in aquaria are *B. aggregatus, B. doriae* (*nunus*) and *B. xanthozona.* Eggs are laid in caves and are guarded by the male.

Family Mastacembelidae

COMMON NAME:	**Fire Eel.**
SCIENTIFIC NAME:	*Mastacembelus erythrotaenia.*
SYNONYM:	*Mastacembelus argus.*
SIZE:	Around 65 cm (26 in), usually smaller.
RANGE:	Thailand to Borneo.
NATURAL HABITAT:	Variety of waters, often with a sandy bed.
WATER CONDITIONS:	Not critical. Temperature 22–28°C (71.5–82°F).
DIET:	Livefoods, particularly bottom-living types, are preferred.
NOTES:	The Fire Eel and other Mastacembelids are commonly referred to as Spiny Eels. All species spend considerable time buried under the gravel and are predominantly nocturnal.

Indian Glass Fish

Bumblebee, Golden Banded Goby

Fire Eel

Selection of Plant Species for the Tropical Aquarium

Setting the Scene

The range of plants available for use in tropical aquaria is steadily increasing. New plants are regularly appearing in a variety of forms, ranging from simple, unrooted cuttings to fully established, container-grown specimens. Among the newer introductions are many plants which are not truly aquatic and will, therefore, die after a longer or shorter period of submergence. While they last, though (and this can be many months) they can add beauty, elegance and shelter to an aquarium. Once they start to deteriorate, it is a good idea to keep a close check on water conditions and replace the plants if any danger signals are spotted, e.g. drop in oxygen concentration if the aquarium is heavily stocked with simultaneously decomposing non-aquatic plants. The species selected in the following pages are all common, mostly aquatic and can survive indefinitely underwater (even though some may occasionally produce stems, leaves or flowers that rise above the water surface). Species have been selected from the following major groups:

Mosses and Liverworts– Bryophytes
Ferns   – Pteridophytes
Flowering plants   – Angiosperms

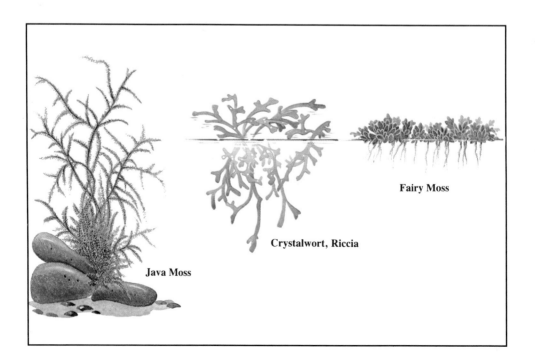

Fairy Moss

Crystalwort, Riccia

Java Moss

Mosses and Liverworts – Bryophytes

Family Hypnaceae

COMMON NAME:	**Java Moss.**
SCIENTIFIC NAME:	*Vesicularia dubyana.*
SYNONYM:	*Hypnum dubyanum.*
RANGE:	India, Indonesia, Southeast Asia.
NATURAL HABITAT:	Often found above water in moist places.
CULTIVATION:	Water and lighting conditions not critical. Temperature 10–30°C (50–86°F).
NOTES:	This species forms an attractive, dense mass of fine shoots which are an ideal shelter for fry and a spawning medium for many species of fish. Some shoots will attach themselves to rocks and aquarium ornaments.

Family Ricciaceae

COMMON NAMES:	**Crystalwort, Riccia.**
SCIENTIFIC NAME:	*Riccia fluitans.*
SYNONYM:	*Ricciella fluitans.*
RANGE:	Widely distributed in tropical and subtropical regions.
NATURAL HABITAT:	Still waters and marshes.
CULTIVATION:	Excessive water hardness should be avoided. Bright illumination is required. Temperature 8–30°C (46–86°F).
NOTES:	*Riccia* forms dense interweaving floating mats on the water surface which provide ideal shelter for fry.

Ferns – Pteridophytes

Family Azollaceae

COMMON NAME:	**Fairy Moss** (but it is a fern).
SCIENTIFIC NAME:	*Azolla caroliniana.*
SYNONYMS:	*Azolla densa, A. mexicana.*
RANGE:	Originally widely distributed in the southern parts of North America and down into South America, but has been introduced into Europe.
NATURAL HABITAT:	Still waters.
CULTIVATION:	Excessive water hardness should be avoided. Bright illumination is required. Temperature 19°C (66°F) in winter, 22°C (71.5°F) and over in summer.
NOTES:	*Azolla* is a floating plant which can form dense carpets in bright light. It can, therefore, deprive submerged plants of the light they require for survival.

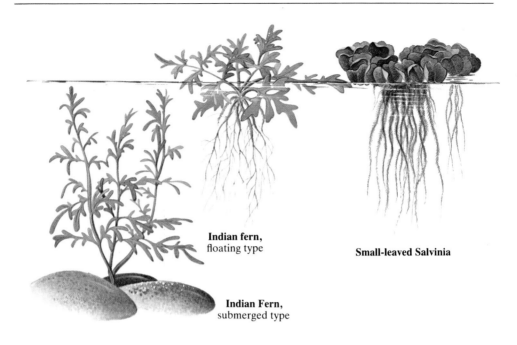

Indian fern,
floating type

Small-leaved Salvinia

Indian Fern,
submerged type

Family Parkeriaeceae

COMMON NAMES: | **Indian Fern, Water Sprite.**
SCIENTIFIC NAME: | *Ceratopteris thalictroides.*
SYNONYM: | *Ceratopteris cornuta* (see Notes).
RANGE: | Most tropical regions.
NATURAL HABITAT: | Still or slow-flowing waters, or even growing on banks.
CULTIVATION: | Soft to medium-hard water with good illumination. Temperature 19–30°c (66–86°F).
NOTES: | Floating leaves are broad while submerged ones are finely divided. Fronds may be 25 cm (9.8 in) long. *C. cornuta* is regarded by some to be a separate species in view of its reduced ability to grow as a submerged plant.

Family Salviniaceae

COMMON NAME: | **Small-leaved Salvinia.**
SCIENTIFIC NAME: | *Salvinia auriculata.*
SYNONYM: | None.
RANGE: | South America.
NATURAL HABITAT: | Still or slow-flowing waters.
CULTIVATION: | Excessively hard water should be avoided. Bright illumination is required. Temperature 18–28°c (64.5–82°F).
NOTES: | The plant's roots are, in fact, finely divided, submerged leaves. Aerial leaves form a hairy mat on the water surface.

Water Wisteria   **Indian Water Star**

Flowering Plants – Angiosperms

Family Acanthaceae

COMMON NAME: **Water Wisteria.**

SCIENTIFIC NAME: *Hygrophila difformis.*

SYNONYMS: *Adenosma triflorum, Synnema triflorum.*

RANGE: Tropical parts of Asia.

NATURAL HABITAT: Variety of waters.

CULTIVATION: Soft water with a sandy bottom. Bright illumination is essential. Temperature 24–28°c (75–82°f) or a little higher.

NOTES: Bunches of this species are particularly attractive. The shape of the leaves is very variable.

COMMON NAME: **Indian Water Star.**

SCIENTIFIC NAME: *Hygrophila polysperma.*

SYNONYMS: *Hemiadelphis polysperma, Justica polysperma.*

RANGE: India.

NATURAL HABITAT: Still waters and marshes.

CULTIVATION: Soft to medium hard water with a coarse sand/fine gravel bottom. Bright illumination is essential. Temperature 18–30°c (64.5–86°f).

NOTES: This is a very popular plant which looks best when grown in clumps.

Amazon Sword Plant

*Aponogeton
ulvaceus*

Family Alismataceae

COMMON NAME: **Amazon Sword Plant.**

SCIENTIFIC NAME: *Echinodorus berteroi.*

SYNONYMS: *Echinodorus cordifolius, E. rostratus, Alisma rostratum.*

RANGE: Southern USA to Central America and the West Indies.

NATURAL HABITAT: Still and slow-flowing waters which may dry out.

CULTIVATION: Water conditions not critical but a bed of coarse sand/fine gravel with an organic component is beneficial. Good to medium light is required. Temperature 20–28°c (68–82°F).

NOTES: *A. berteroi* forms a good specimen plant with leaves that can measure up to 80 cm (32 in), but usually considerably less in aquaria. Other species of Amazon Sword include *E. bleheri* (*E. paniculatus*), *E. latifolius* (*E. intermedius* or *magdalenensis* – the Dwarf Amazon Sword), *E. tenellus* (*E. parvulus* or *subulatus* or *Alisma tenellum* – the Junior or Pygmy Chain Amazon Sword).

Family Aponogetonaceae

COMMON NAME: None.

SCIENTIFIC NAME: *Aponogeton ulvaceus.*

SYNONYM: None.

RANGE: Malagasy.

NATURAL HABITAT: Still and flowing waters.

CULTIVATION: Soft, acid water with an organically rich rooting medium. Good illumination required for this species. Temperature 20–28°c (68–82°F) during growing period; somewhat lower during resting period when the leaves begin to die back. Leaves may be up to 35 cm (14 in) long.

NOTES: *Aponogeton* species grow from corms which normally experience a resting period of several months. Other species available include *A. crispus, A. echinatus, A. elongatus, A. fenestralis* and *A. undulatus.*

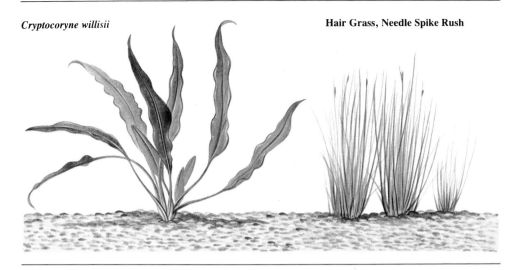

Cryptocoryne willisii   **Hair Grass, Needle Spike Rush**

Family Araceae

COMMON NAME:	None.
SCIENTIFIC NAME:	***Cryptocoryne willisii.***
SYNONYMS:	*Cryptocoryne pseudobeckettii, C. undulata.*
RANGE:	Sri Lanka.
NATURAL HABITAT:	Marshy areas.
CULTIVATION:	Soft, acid water combined with coarse sand or fine gravel with a rich organic component is best. Will grow quite adequately at medium light levels. Temperature around 26°C (79°F).
NOTES:	Numerous species of *Cryptocoryne* are available and, while the above holds true for many of these, individual requirements should be checked in specialist literature or with specialist growers. Some species available are: *C. affinis* (*haerteliana*), *C. balansae* (*C. somphongsii*), *C. beckettii, C. ciliata* (*C. elata, Ambrosinia ciliata, Lagenandra ovata*), *C. cordata* (*C. grandis*), *C. griffithii, C. lutea, C. nevillii, C. purpurea, C. wendtii.* Crypts look particularly good when grown in clumps.

Family Cyperaceae

COMMON NAMES:	**Hair Grass, Needle Spike Rush.**
SCIENTIFIC NAME:	*Eleocharis acicularis.*
SYNONYMS:	*Heleocharis acicularis, Scirpus radicans.*
RANGE:	Widespread in subtropical and temperate zones.
NATURAL HABITAT:	Often in moist non-submerged areas.
CULTIVATION:	Water conditions not critical as long as extremes are avoided. A sandy bottom and relatively cool temperatures are preferred, 22°C (71.5°F). Good to medium light recommended.
NOTES:	This species does best in tropical aquaria when it is allowed to acclimatise gradually to higher temperatures.

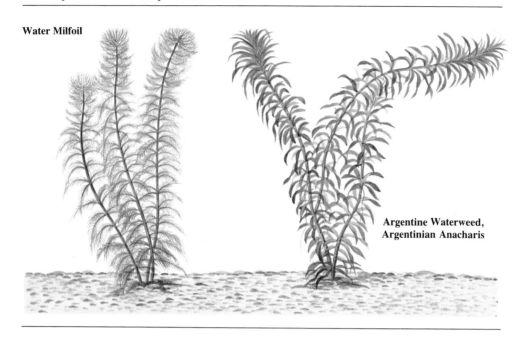

Water Milfoil

**Argentine Waterweed,
Argentinian Anacharis**

Family Halorrhagaceae

COMMON NAME: **Water Milfoil.**

SCIENTIFIC NAME: *Myrophyllum* spp.

SYNONYM: Many species are known or presumed and nomenclature is unclear.

RANGE: Widely distributed in tropical, subtropical and temperate zones.

NATURAL HABITAT: Still and flowing waters.

CULTIVATION: Neutral to alkaline, hard water with sandy bottom and an organic component. Bright illumination is essential. Temperature up to 25°C (77°F).

NOTES: Milfoils are popular fine-leaved plants which provide shelter for fry and a spawning medium for egg scatterers when grown in clumps.

Family Hydrocharitaceae

COMMON NAMES: **Argentine Waterweed, Argentinian Anacharis.**

SCIENTIFIC NAME: *Egeria densa.*

SYNONYMS: *Anacharis densa, Elodea densa.*

RANGE: Eastern parts of South America, but widely introduced elsewhere.

NATURAL HABITAT: Wide variety of waters, from ponds to rivers.

CULTIVATION: Water conditions are not critical but medium hard water with a sandy bottom is suitable. Good illumination is essential. Temperature 12–28°C (53–82°F).

NOTES: This species is often confused with similar ones such as *Elodea canadensis* which is generally darker and has smaller leaves, 1 cm ($\frac{1}{2}$ in) compared to 2–3 cm (about 1 in), and *Lagarosiphon major* which is more robust and luxuriant and is often called 'Crispa' by pondkeepers.

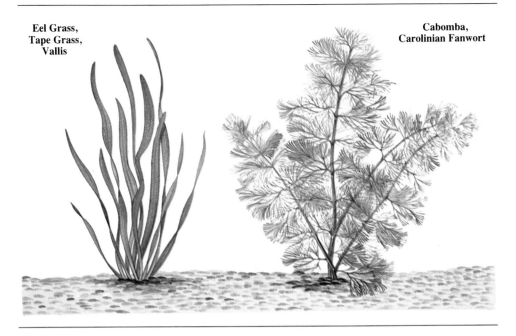

**Eel Grass,
Tape Grass,
Vallis**

**Cabomba,
Carolinian Fanwort**

COMMON NAMES:	**Eel Grass, Tape Grass, Vallis.**
SCIENTIFIC NAME:	*Vallisneria spiralis.*
SYNONYMS:	*Vallisneria* 'Torta' (corkscrew variety) and numerous others.
RANGE:	Widespread in tropical and subtropical zones.
NATURAL HABITAT:	Clear, still and flowing waters.
CULTIVATION:	Water conditions are not critical but medium-hard conditions with a sandy bottom and a small amount of organic matter are preferred. Bright illumination is essential. Temperature 10–30°c (50–86°F).
NOTES:	This is a prolific plant which reproduces predominantly by means of runners. Other species and varieties available include: *V. americana, V. gigantea, V. spiralis* var. *tortifolia, V. spiralis* 'Contortionist' and *V. neotropicalis.*

Family Nymphaeaceae

COMMON NAMES:	**Cabomba, Carolinian Fanwort.**
SCIENTIFIC NAME:	*Cabomba caroliniana.*
SYNONYMS:	*Cabomba peltata, C. pinnata, Nectris peltata.*
RANGE:	Southern USA.
NATURAL HABITAT:	Shallow, still and slow-flowing waters.
CULTIVATION:	Soft water preferred with coarse sandy bottom enriched with loam or other suitable organic medium. Good illumination is required. Temperature 18–28°c (64.5–82°F).
NOTES:	Stems can grow to 150 cm (5 ft) in length. Dense clumps afford good shelter for fry and a good spawning medium for egg scatterers.

Ludwigia natans   *Bacopa monnieri*

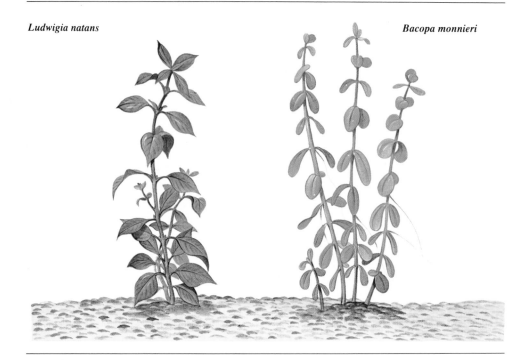

Family Onagraceae

COMMON NAME: None.

SCIENTIFIC NAME: ***Ludwigia natans*** (see Notes).

SYNONYM: *Ludwigia mulertii.*

RANGE: Southern States of USA, Central America.

NATURAL HABITAT: Still or slow-flowing waters.

CULTIVATION: Excessively hard water must be avoided. Sandy bottom with an organic component, and a good illumination are recommended. Temperature 18–25°c (64.5–77°f).

NOTES: This species is believed to be a hybrid between *L. palustris* and *L. repens* by some. Whatever the case, this plant looks magnificent when grown in clumps.

Family Scrophulariaceae

COMMON NAME: None.

SCIENTIFIC NAME: ***Bacopa monnieri.***

SYNONYMS: *Herpestes monnieria, Lysimachia monnieri.*

RANGE: All tropical and subtropical regions.

NATURAL HABITAT: Still shallow waters and marshes.

CULTIVATION: Excessively hard water should be avoided. Coarse sand or fine gravel are suitable rooting media. Good (but not excessive) illumination is required. Temperature 15–26°c (59–79°f).

NOTES: Aerial leaves may be produced in shallow water if growth is healthy.

Bibliography

Reference Works Relating to Classification

Greenwood, P.H., Rosen, D.E., Weitzman, S.H. and Myers, G.: *Phyletic Studies of Teleostean Fishes, with a Provisional Classification of Living Forms.* Bulletin of the American Museum of Natural History, Volume 131: Article 4, 1966

Nelson, J.S.: *Fishes of the World.* John Wiley & Sons, 1976.

Parenti, L.R.: *A Phylogenetic and Biogeographic Analysis of Cyprinodontiform Fishes (Teleostei, Atherinomorpha).* Bulletin of the American Museum of Natural History, Volume 168: Article 4, 1981.

Rosen, D.E. and Bailey, R.M.: *The Poeciliid Fishes (Cyprinodontiformes), their Structure, Zoogeography and Systematics.* Bulletin of the American Museum of Natural History, Volume 126: Article 1. 1963.

Aquarium Reference Books

Axelrod, H.R., et al: *Exotic Tropical Fishes* (Looseleaf Edition). T.F.H. Publications, Inc. (publishers of *Tropical Fish Hobbyist* magazine).

Dawes, J.A.: *The Freshwater Aquarium: Questions and Answers.* Robert Royce Ltd., 1984.

Hervey, G.F. and Hems, J.: *A Guide to Freshwater Aquarium Fishes.* Hamlyn, 1983.

Hunnan, P., Milne, A. Stebbing, P.: *The Living Aquarium.* Ward Lock Ltd., 1981.

Mayland, H.J. (Translated by Vevers, G.): *The Complete Home Aquarium.* Ward Lock Ltd., 1976.

Mills, R. (Dick): *Illustrated Guide to Aquarium Fishes.* Kingfisher Books Ltd., 1981.

Paysan, K.: *Country Life Guide to Aquarium Fishes.* Newnes Books, 1975.

van Ramshorst, J.D. (Ed.): *The Complete Aquarium Encyclopaedia of Tropical Freshwater Fish.* Elsevier–Phaidon, 1978.

Index